Choosing Peace

A Handbook on War, Peace, and Your Conscience

by Robert A. Seeley

Central Committee for Conscientious Objectors

Philadelphia   *San Francisco*

September, 1994

ISBN 0-933368-07-0

Cover design by Felicity Productions.
Cover graphic by Daniel McClain.

Printing History

First Edition: September, 1994—5,000 copies

Central Committee for Conscientious Objectors

2208 South Street   655 Sutter Street, Ste. 514
Philadelphia, PA 19146   San Francisco, CA 94102
215-545-4626   415-474-3002
Fax 215-546-2368   Fax 415-474-2311

For Jim Bristol

Who chose peace and lived it all his life.

Foreword

This book began as a revision of the *Handbook for Conscientious Objectors,* CCCO's guide for civilian conscientious objectors. Long acknowledged as an essential tool for men facing the draft, the *Handbook* would have celebrated its 45th anniversary in 1994. Instead, after a good deal of evolution and rethinking, it has become the book you are now reading. Its title, arrangement, and emphasis are so different from the older *Handbook* that it seemed inappropriate to retain the traditional title even though this book shares many chapters with the 13th Edition of its predecessor.

How, then, is this book different from the traditional *Handbook for Conscientious Objectors?* And why must it be different?

In 1949, CCCO published a brief pamphlet titled "Conscientious Objectors Under the Draft Law." Within a few months, this pamphlet had grown until, when it was time for a second printing, it had become a book— the first *Handbook for Conscientious Objectors.* Like all subsequent editions of the *Handbook,* the new book was a practical guide to applying for conscientious objector status under the draft; protecting oneself against local draft boards which were then (as always) hostile, arbitrary, and ignorant of the law; and navigating the maze of draft regulations and appeal procedures. A brief section discussed the practical meaning of key legal terms such as "religious training and belief." Much of this material was challenging and thought-provoking, but its focus was on legal requirements, not on religious, philosophical, and moral issues in themselves.

As CCCO's understanding of draft law grew, and as the law on conscientious objection evolved, the *Handbook* put more emphasis on guiding the reader through Selective Service procedures and less emphasis on broader questions. There was still much thoughtful material on religion, the use of force, and other issues, but these were still considered solely in the context of the law's requirements. As time went on CCCO published separate pamphlets on broader issues (e.g., "So You Would Fight if the Country Were Attacked?" in 1968) rather than incorporating this material into the *Handbook*.

In 1972, the *Handbook for Conscientious Objectors* went into its 12th Edition. Inductions under the draft ended in December of that year, and the induction authority expired on July 1, 1973. The *Handbook*, with its emphasis on coping with an active draft, went into sudden eclipse, and was not again published until 1981, when CCCO revived it to meet the revival of draft registration and the threat of renewed inductions.

By 1980, when I took over editorship of the *Handbook*, the political and military situations had changed, and it was clear that the older approaches would no longer serve. Many potential *Handbook* readers knew little about conscientious objection and the variety of moral issues surrounding it. A new book which did not speak directly about these moral issues risked becoming irrelevant or at least less than useful to its readers.

The 13th Edition *Handbook* also had a new author with a different approach from that of previous authors. My own emphasis in counseling had always been on moral rather than technical issues, and I had apprenticed for the writing of the new book by a ten-year self-education in military history and military affairs. It was clear to me that this background could enrich the *Handbook*—but only if the new edition went beyond technical questions and addressed moral issues directly. Even the style of the book had to change to include women, who might become subject to a future draft, as well as men.

I therefore reorganized the book and rewrote it from scratch. Among other changes, for the first time the 13th Edition *Handbook* included chapters designed specifically to challenge the reader's thinking on war. There were chapters on Hitler, the use of force, and similar issues, along with a long, free-form chapter that discussed the nature of war. Because the inclusion of this material represented a major change from older *Handbooks,* we decided to introduce them with a special note to the reader which made clear that one did not have to agree with them or even read them to be a conscientious objector. This "apology" has proven to be unnecessarily cautious, and over the years many readers have found that these new chapters were, for them, actually the core of the book.

By the time of the Persian Gulf War, in 1990-1991, CCCO's stocks of the *Handbook* were very low, and a new edition would have become necessary shortly, war or no war. The War at first increased the urgency of the revision, but when it ended after less than two months of actual combat, we quickly realized that a mere update of the 13th Edition *Handbook* would be inadequate. The Gulf War had demonstrated, as little else could, that a full-scale U.S. mobilization for war was unlikely. The details of the mobilization draft, so central to the 13th Edition of the *Handbook,* were therefore less important than full discussion of the issues which military-age people face as they make decisions about war in their lives.

Except for Selective Service registration, those issues do not include the draft—but they are real and pressing nonetheless. The military and war have not gone away; their intrusion into our lives has instead assumed new forms. This book therefore, for the first time in a CCCO book, discusses military recruitment and the choices (and pitfalls) which it presents to young people. For the first time we have included a chapter, "Choosing Peace in a Warlike World," that is designed to help readers live out their beliefs; it includes suggestions for small and large actions that readers might consider—from volunteering at a local community center to refusing military taxes.

Chapters on Selective Service registration, which readers still need, are here also, as is a detailed description of the mobilization draft. This material, however, is no longer central to the book, and its position in the table of contents reflects this change.

The central difference between this book and the older *Handbook for Conscientious Objectors*—and the reason why we have decided to change its title and begin a new tradition—is its emphasis on conscientious objection as a moral question with many answers. CCCO has long believed that the law's definition of conscientious objection is too narrow. This book puts that belief into practice. Readers who do not qualify as conscientious objectors under the law will, I hope, find here much to interest and challenge them. It is my firm belief that everyone—those who oppose all wars, those who oppose particular wars, and those who support some uses of military force—has a part to play in building a better world. In that better world, war and the military will have a smaller role than they do today. If this book helps readers to define their part in creating a more positive future, it will have done its job.

This book carries my by-line, and I am ultimately responsible for what is said in it. No book, however, is completely the work of one person. I am grateful to many individuals and groups for their help, both direct and indirect, in completing this challenging and rewarding project.

First and foremost, though too late for him to read it, I am grateful to James E. Bristol for his support through the years and specifically for his strong support of the concepts underlying this book. When I proposed a radical revision of the older *Handbook for Conscientious Objectors,* Jim was the first to call me with his enthusiastic support of the project. I wish that I could present him with the first copy.

In preparing the material in these chapters, I have drawn on many sources. Most important for me have been the works of John Keegan, Gwynne Dyer, Lyn Macdonald, Alistair Horne, Aldous Huxley, and Jonathan Schell. I am grateful to Murray Polner of Lakewood Press, who commissioned me to prepare the *Handbook of Non-Violence*, thereby providing the first opportunity for me to write at length about some of the issues in the present book.

Thanks are also due to Dee Bristol, who read and approved the first chapter's discussion of her husband, Jim; to the CCCO Board, which approved the concept of this book and gave me a free hand in realizing it; to Anne Toensmeier, who proofread the galleys; to Diane Smith, Allen Nelson, and Alex Doty of the CCCO staff; and to my wife and daughter, without whose support I probably could not have done such a major project. Among those who read the manuscript and contributed either directly or indirectly to what follows are L. William Yolton, Sam Diener, Karen Jewett, James Feldman, Jr., Peter Goldberger, and Carlos Lezama. To all these people, and to others whom I have inadvertently omitted, I owe more than I can say.

—Robert A. Seeley
June 13, 1994

Contents

Part I

Getting Started

Chapter 1
What This Book Can Do For You

In 1940, Jim Bristol was pastor of a Lutheran Church in Camden, New Jersey. When Congress passed the first peacetime draft law,* Jim could have applied for exemption as a minister. After much thought and prayer, he chose not to do so. He had rejected war in his own life, and it would be inconsistent, he felt, to sign up for a draft system that would soon be sending others off to fight. He decided not to register for the draft at all.

As a result of his stand, Jim Bristol served eighteen months in federal prison. But his time in prison was not the end of his career; it was the beginning. He went on

---

* Author's Note: Throughout this book, I use the term "draft" to mean a process by which the government orders some (or all) of its physically able citizens to perform military duty for a period of time. Another word for this process is "conscription." A "draft law" is a law which gives the government the power to compel its citizens to enter the military. In the United States, the draft law is the Military Selective Service Act (MSSA). Although the government's authority to draft people expired in 1973, the MSSA remains in force. It is administered by the Selective Service System. When you register with Selective Service, as described later in this book, your name joins a list of men who could be called to military duty in an emergency. In other words, you are registering for the draft.

to serve on the staff of the American Friends Service Committee, an international humanitarian organization, for over 25 years, and to devote his life to the search for peace and justice. He worked in India and in Southern Africa; he served on the boards of CCCO and many other groups. He and his wife, Dee, hosted Martin and Coretta King on their visit to India in 1959.

By the time of his death in 1992, Jim Bristol had changed thousands of lives directly and hundreds of thousands indirectly. But he wasn't a saint, and he wasn't Superman. He was a homeowner with a family who drove a modest car, ate an ordinary diet, and loved sports all his life. He could and did lose his temper. And he always thought of himself as an ordinary person doing what his conscience told him to do.

Conscientious Objection and Your Life

Not everyone can be a Jim Bristol. But each of us can decide for ourselves whether we can be part of war, what we think about violence, and what that means for our lives. For Jim Bristol, the search for peace became central. Your decision about war may lead you in a different direction. That is how it should be. It is *your* decision, not someone else's. This book will explain what conscientious objection is. It will help you to decide where you stand on war. And it will help you think about what you should do once you've decided.

Over the years, there have been many kinds of conscientious objectors. Some, like Jim Bristol, opposed all wars. Others opposed only the war they were asked to fight in. Still others refused to follow military orders which they thought were wrong. And many resisted without filling out a form or telling anyone what they were doing. They simply did not register for the draft or, if they were soldiers, went absent without leave.

These people had one thing in common. All felt that war or some part of war was evil. All believed this so strongly that they could not do what they felt was wrong. Each CO, soldier or civilian, man or woman, drew a different line. But all by their actions said, "I cannot do this because it is wrong."

This book is about the lines which you will have to draw as a person who has to make choices about the military—whether or not you ever face the draft.

But Why Think About It ?

If you're subject to draft registration you may not need much argument on why you should think about war. Even though you may never be drafted, registration can make you think about where you stand because you have to.

But like all things connected with war and peace it isn't always that simple. Conscientious objection isn't just a classification under the draft. It's a moral question which you face every day whether you think about it or not. The military hasn't gone away because nobody is being drafted. You've probably already gotten mailings or phone calls from military recruiters, but if you haven't, chances are you will. You can throw them into the trash or recycle them, but when you do so, you aren't just cleaning up clutter. You're making a decision about whether to be part of war. And the more you learn about these issues, the better your decision will be.

There's another reason to think about war and peace.

No matter where you come out on these issues you are going to be a citizen of this country and the world. You'll probably vote in the future. And when nuclear war could wipe out civilization, your vote will be important not just for the country but for everyone in the world. If you decide now where you stand on war your vote will mean that much more. And if you want to make a more peaceful world you can do it best by knowing where you stand and why.

If you ever *are* drafted, you won't have much time. "The Mobilization Draft," in the Appendix of this book explains how an emergency draft might work. You'll notice that you might have as little as ten days to make up your mind whether or not you're a conscientious objector. That's not much time. You wouldn't want to have to decide whether to get married in such a short time. And deciding about war is just that hard. Your decision can change your life for better or worse. It might even lead you to resist the draft and risk a prison term.

What Is a Conscientious Objector?

In Chapters 3 and 4 of this book you'll find a discussion of the legal definition of conscientious objection. Under U.S. law, a CO is a person who objects to "participation in war in any form"—i.e., to all wars—because of his or her religious or moral beliefs. Over the years the courts have defined these words very precisely, but the basic government requirements for COs, that they object to all wars because of their religious or moral beliefs, haven't changed very much. If you ever face the draft, you'll need to think about whether you qualify as a conscientious objector. But our law isn't the last word on conscientious objection. Conscientious objection isn't just a provision of law. It's a moral position that can change your life. We need a better definition of it than what the law gives.

That's why, except when it is talking about the law, this book will use a different definition of conscientious objection. For this book, a conscientious objector will be anyone who objects to war or some part of war so strongly that he or she cannot be part of it. CCCO believes that the law's definition of conscientious objection is too narrow. It leaves out many people who have taken thoughtful and powerful stands against war. As you think about war in your own life, don't think only about what the law requires. Think about what *your* beliefs are and what they mean for you.

People of Color

War is no respecter of race. In the First World War most of those killed were white Europeans. Millions of Japanese, Chinese, and Southeast Asian people died in World War II. And an "enemy" can become a friend very quickly depending on the world situation—just as Germany and Japan did after World War II.

But it's also true that the wars since World War II have taken place mainly in the Third World. In Korea (1950-1953), Vietnam (1953-1975), and the Persian Gulf War (1991), U.S. troops fought against people of color. France fought non-white peoples in Algeria (1954) and Indochina (1947-1953). And the Soviet Union invaded a Third World country when it sent troops into Afghanistan (1979-1985).

The U.S. military draws many recruits from the unemployed. And a great many unemployed are people of color. In the military itself people of color have less opportunity than whites and most officers are whites. Some of this is caused by racism and some by the military structure.

The whole question of war, racism and the military is very complex. This book deals with it briefly in Chapter 13, but to understand how the military treats people of color, you'll need more information than you'll find there. The list of books under "Further Reading" can give you a start.

Do you think wars against Third World countries are wrong? Or do you oppose any wars? Do you think the many wars against Third World countries in the last thirty years are an accident? Or are they too a result of the war system? And what does this mean for you and your life? You are the only one who can decide.

What About Women?

Women are not now covered by the draft law. They don't have to register and they can't be drafted. But Congress or the courts could very quickly change the law to make it cover women. Many people think women should be drafted under a future draft.

As a woman, even though you're not now subject to the draft, you'll almost certainly get calls and letters from military recruiters. The Pentagon relies heavily on women to fill its ranks. So you too have to decide how you feel about the military.

Women in the military have many problems—discrimination, sexual harassment, and rape, among others. This book discusses them briefly in Chapter 13, but to get more information you should start with some of the books under "Further Reading."

What this book is primarily about is war. And that's an issue you would face even if the military were the perfect place for women.

How To Use This Book

No book is a substitute for good counseling. If you're confused about anything you need to talk to someone who knows about conscientious objection. CCCO can help you find good counseling. And it's best to have counseling even if you're not confused.

But you can use this book to do two things: to learn about war and decide where you stand; and to decide how to act on your stand once you've made it.

Part I of this book, which you're reading now, gives you an idea what is in the book and explains the steps you can take to protect yourself if you are considering enlisting in the military, or if you ever face the draft.

Part II explains the law on conscientious objection and war resistance. You don't have to qualify as a conscientious objector to choose peace, but these chapters will help you focus and get started on thinking about these issues.

In Part III you'll find chapters on some of the questions you might want to think about as you decide where you stand. This Part gives you some background on the U.S. military. It discusses the ways we use the military and some of the reasons that strategists now use to justify wars. And it talks about some of the questions you may face—from yourself, from your friends, or from a local draft board—as you decide whether you are a conscientious objector. You probably won't agree with everything in these chapters, and that's good. Your opinion, not what's in this book, is what counts. These chapters are designed to start you thinking—no matter where you finally come out.

Part IV of this book is about choices you face right now. It discusses military recruitment—how it works, and some issues concerning it that you may face each day. It discusses ways you can live by your beliefs, including a brief discussion of what is likely to happen to the draft in the future. Finally, this section contains a personal note to parents from the author.

Part V will help you to understand the decisions you need to make now if you're subject to draft registration, and how to prepare yourself to make a future CO claim. Although no civilian COs have been jailed since the early 1980s, it's useful to know the worst that the government could do to you and how to deal with the authorities if they decide to investigate or charge you with a federal crime. So this section includes a brief discussion of legal penalties for refusing to register with Selective Service.

At the end of many chapters in this book, you'll find some questions you might want to think about. You don't have to answer all these questions in order to be a conscientious objector, but you may find them helpful as you think about your beliefs. Some chapters also have a list of ideas for research topics for school assignments. Not every chapter has these lists. If you find them helpful, tell us. We'd like to know.

The Appendix to this book contains a description of

the mobilization draft and how it would work if it came back tomorrow. This section is mainly of interest to people who might face a future draft, but if you want to know what might happen in a mobilization, you should read it.

At the back of this book you'll also find two reading lists. The first, "A Short Course on War and Peace," is designed to get you started if you want to explore these issues further. The second, "Further Reading" is a more complete list that you can use for researching papers, browsing, or whatever you wish. And of course you can always get more information from CCCO.

Good luck!

Chapter 2
Protecting Yourself

There are many steps you can take now which will help if you face conscription of any kind in the future. If you or your friends are considering military enlistment, you should also take steps to protect yourself. Most of these precautions are simple. This chapter summarizes a set of good habits for conscientious objectors—and for anyone else who must make choices about war.

Good Habits for COs and Others

General Precautions

✔ *Make all requests, appeals, and claims in writing.* An oral request is worthless if the government denies you made it; they can't deny that you made a written request if you keep good records.

✔ *Keep copies* of everything you send to Selective Service, a recruiting command, or other Federal agencies. This applies also to letters to other government agencies—like a request to your school board for a speaker on peace at your school.

✔ *Keep good records.* Your records don't have to be elaborate, but it's important that you know where you can locate copies of your Selective Service or CO documents.

✔ *Use certified mail, return receipt requested, for all correspondence with Selective Service.* That way you'll know that the government received your letters and your registration form. If there's any question, you will have the receipts.

Preparing Yourself

✔ *Keep informed:* CCCO's *News Notes* covers conscientious objection, the law, Selective Service, and other issues. It's available free to contributors or others who need it. Details on draft and military law will be found in *The Objector,* CCCO's magazine for counselors. For information on subscriptions, contact CCCO-Western Region. CCCO can help you find counseling on conscientious objection, military recruitment, Selective Service registration, the military Delayed Entry Program, and military discharges if you need it.

✔ *Decide where you stand:* This book tries to help you make good decisions about war. You may decide that you are a conscientious objector, or you may take some other stand on war. Either way, if you face conscription in the future, knowing where you stand will help you.

✔ *Keep thinking:* No decision that you make now is forever. As you learn more about war and peace, you'll find that your thinking changes.

✔ *Talk about your beliefs with people who are COs, and with people who are not.* Many times you can learn a great deal about yourself by talking with somebody who disagrees with you.

✔ *Consider counseling other young people on their options.*

CCCO can train you in pre-enlistment, military, and draft counseling. Contact the CCCO office nearest you for information.

If You Think You Might Be a CO...

✔ *Build a record:* Selective Service won't process any claim for deferment or exemption right now. But you can get your views and your claims on record as suggested in Chapter 18 of this book.

✔ *Avoid Junior ROTC or other military programs:* If you're thinking about becoming a CO, your having been part of the military could cause problems for you. It's best to avoid involvement with the military until you've decided that you're definitely *not* a CO. And there are lots of good reasons to avoid these programs anyway.

If You Or Your Friends Visit a Recruiter...

✔ *Don't talk with the recruiter alone.* Take someone with you as a witness.

✔ *Never give false information to the recruiter.* If a recruiter asks you to falsify information about your record or any other matter, say no. Falsifying information in order to enlist is a crime under military law, and if you're court-martialed it will be your word against that of the recruiter.

✔ *Don't sign any documents until you've taken them home and studied them.* This would apply to any legal transaction, but it's doubly important with military enlistment documents.

✔ *Keep copies of all documents.* Again, this applies to any legal transaction.

✔ *Accept no oral promises.* Remember, if what the

recruiter promised isn't in your written agreement, it is worthless.

✔ *Talk with people who have been in the military before you decide.* Some people had a good experience; others had a bad one. Try to find people who had both.

If There Is a Draft...

✔ *Do not rely on promises from local board clerks or members or from other draft officials.* Unless you object to doing so, follow the printed instructions on all forms. If you don't understand the instructions, get help from CCCO or a draft counselor. If you talk with a draft official on the telephone, get the official's name and write a letter to Selective Service confirming in writing what you were told on the telephone.

✔ *Present as full a case as possible* to your local board, even if you think the board is hostile and will disregard everything you say. Your local board may turn out to be more fair than you thought, or, if not, having your full case on record can help you on appeal or in court.

✔ *Follow deadlines.* Your requests for new classifications and appeals must meet strict deadlines. You must *postmark* your reply by the deadline or risk losing your appeal or your chance for a different classification.

✔ *If you're away from home,* arrange for someone to look at your mail and contact you at once if you receive any notice from Selective Service. If you're abroad, leave behind a signed request for an appeal for your mail-opener to date and forward.

✔ *When in doubt, get help.* CCCO can help you to find a draft counselor or an attorney if you need one.

Part II

Conscientious Objectors and the Law

Chapter 3
Conscientious Objection Under the Law

In order to decide whether you're a conscientious objector, you need to think about war and what you believe. This chapter explains the law on conscientious objection, but knowing the law isn't enough. In fact, the law can sometimes confuse the issue more than it helps. Before you decide whether you fit under the law, you need to think about where you fit into the war system—if you do at all. That's what the rest of this book should help you to do.

The basic law on conscientious objection is in Section 6(j) of the Military Selective Service Act, which provides exemption for conscientious objectors to war. It reads in part:

> Nothing contained in this [Act] shall ... require any person to be subject to combatant training and service in the Armed Forces of the United States who, by reason of religious training and belief, is conscientiously opposed to participation in war in any form. As used in this subsection, the term "religious training and belief" does not include essentially political, sociological, or philosophical views, or a merely personal moral code. Any person claiming exemption from combatant training and service because of such conscientious objection whose claim is sustained by the local board shall, if he is

inducted into the Armed Forces under this [Act], be assigned to noncombatant service ... or shall, if he is found to be conscientiously opposed to such noncombatant service, in lieu of induction, be ordered by his local board, subject to such regulations as the President may prescribe, to perform for a period [of two years] ... civilian work contributing to the maintenance of the national health, safety, or interest.

But What Does It Mean?

Section 6(j) is hard even for attorneys and judges to understand. But the basic standards for conscientious objectors are simple. The Supreme Court summarized them in *Clay v. U.S.* (1971). A conscientious objector under the law, the Court said, must:

✔ Be "religious," as the Supreme Court has defined this word (see below);

✔ Object to all wars; and

✔ Be sincere in his or her application.

Your job, if you face the draft and decide to apply for CO status, will be to convince your local board that you meet these standards. If you've made a good application, your local board then can't turn you down unless they have good reasons for doing so. For more information on preparing to make a good claim, see Chapter 18. For more information on the draft procedures as they might work in the a future draft, see Appendix 3 of this book, "The Mobilization Draft."

"Religion" and the Law

To qualify as a conscientious objector, you must base your claim on "religious training and belief." But this doesn't mean you have to be religious *as most of us use that word.* In *U.S. v. Seeger* (1965), the Supreme Court said that a religious belief is "a sincere and meaningful" belief that "occupies a place in the life of its possessor parallel to that filled by [an] orthodox belief in God." You can base your CO claim on a traditional religion, like Christianity, or on some other belief that has the same place in your life. As long as your claim is based on a belief that is central to you, you can qualify as a conscientious objector. Your belief can be religious, moral, or ethical—or a mixture of all three. You don't have to believe in God or attend church. And in a later case, *Welsh v. U.S.* (1970), the Supreme Court said that you don't even have to call your belief religious.

Whether or not you think of yourself as religious, filing for CO status, or thinking about conscientious objection, means thinking about your most important beliefs and feelings. Do you believe in a god? If so, what do you believe about your god? Or about your own place in the world and the universe? Questions like these are important as you decide whether to file for CO status and as you prepare yourself to file.

Even though the law doesn't require a traditional religious claim, it's useful to know what some thinkers have said about religion and its relation to moral choices. Paul Tillich, the well-known Lutheran theologian, spoke of:

> [T]he "God above God," the power of being, which works through those who have no name for it, not even the name God.

John Woolman, a Quaker anti-slavery activist, said:

> There is a principle which is pure, placed in the human mind, which in different places and ages hath had different names.... It is deep and inward, confined to no forms of religion, nor excluded from any.... In whomso-

ever this takes root and grows, of what nation soever, they become brethren.

Religion, say these writers, does not have to be called "religious." Martin Luther King, Jr., added:

It really boils down to this: that all life is interrelated.... Whatever affects one directly, affects all indirectly. We are made to live together because of the interrelated structure of reality.

And David Saville Muzzey, a well-known Ethical Culture thinker, said, "Religion ... must surely mean the devotion of man to the highest idea that he can conceive. "

What is *your* highest ideal? How does it lead you to oppose war? These are questions you need to ask yourself as you think about conscientious objection.

If you're a member of a church, even one of the traditional "peace churches," you still need to think hard about what you believe. Under the law, it's your individual belief, not the beliefs of your church, that counts. When you apply for CO status, it's not enough to say, for instance, that you are a Quaker. And it's not enough to quote your church's creed. How does your creed lead you to be a CO? Even in the "peace churches," many church members join the military. Why not you? You need to know, and, if you apply for CO status, your local board will want to know.

Religious Training

Many COs worry that they won't be able to show any religious training when they apply for CO status. Even if you've never been to church or Sunday School, however, this is less of a problem than you may think. How did you come to your belief? The answer to this question, under the law, is your religious training. Your training is the background to the beliefs you have.

This means that you don't have to show you went to Sunday School unless it affected the way you believe now. You don't have to show anything other than how you came to the belief you have. It's important to think clearly about how you became a CO—both for your local board and for yourself. For ideas on how to show your training, see Chapter 18.

War in Any Form

To qualify as a conscientious objector, you must object to "war in any form." This doesn't mean that you have to oppose all use of force. You have to object to "real shooting wars," wars as common sense uses the word. Any other beliefs you have are important, but they don't have any bearing on your CO claim.

Some COs don't know what they would do in the future—or what they would have done in the past. If you're in this situation, you may still qualify as a CO who objects to "war in any form." During the Vietnam era, many COs applied to their draft boards using an "existential" approach. What, they asked themselves, do I believe here and now? Do I really know that my beliefs will be different in the future? Or can I leave that for the future? These are good questions to ask yourself.

The next chapter explains in more detail what is meant by "war in any form." And if you don't know where you stand on this question, you may find Part III helpful also.

"Deeply Held" Beliefs

COs and local boards are often confused because Selective Service directives say that a CO's beliefs must be both sincere *and* "deeply held. " What does "deeply held" mean? How do you show that your beliefs are "deeply held"? Are some beliefs "deeper" than others?

It's hard to understand, but, luckily, you don't have to. The courts have held that your local board can't deny your claim because your beliefs are not "deeply held" enough. "Depth of conviction," said one court, "requires theological or philosophical speculation. We think it unwise to adopt this more complex concept as the requirement which a Selective Service registrant ... must fulfill in order to qualify for conscientious objector classification."

For purposes of law, sincerity is enough. Are you what you claim to be? That's the only question you need to answer. Your local board can't say that you are what you claim to be but don't feel strongly enough about it.

"No Rest or Peace"

You won't be surprised to learn that the government sometimes uses illegal standards in judging CO claims. The most troublesome of these is the idea that you must prove your conscience would give you "no rest or peace" if you had to take part in war. Courts which have ruled on this standard have said the government can't use it, but you may still find it on the CO form or other Selective Service documents.

You can't prevent the government from using illegal standards. What you can do is to make decisions about war which fit your conscience. And you can decide now not to be intimidated by the "no rest or peace" language. It's illegal for the government to use it, so you can ignore it and concentrate on what you think about war.

Personal Moral Code

Section 6(1) seems to say that you can't be a CO if you oppose war because of a "merely personal moral code." If you have trouble understanding how this is different from a moral objection to war, you're not alone. In philosophy and in the law as interpreted by the courts, there's no real difference between a personal moral code and a moral belief about war.

All moral beliefs are personal. If you believe that you should not be part of war, that's a personal decision, even if you base your decision on your church's teachings. Few churches require their members to be COs. And whether you're a church member or not, war is a matter between you and your conscience. Your CO beliefs are your personal beliefs. But they also qualify as "religious" beliefs if they are central to your life. Keep this in mind, and you won't get confused if your local board says you have a "merely personal moral code."

Political Beliefs

Like most COs or people who are against war, you probably have ideas about politics, U.S. foreign policy, the defense budget, the draft, and many other issues. You may consider your beliefs political—not religious or moral.

But if you object to all war, there's a good chance that you have a belief which qualifies as "religious" under the law. Your local board can't deny your CO claim unless the sole basis for it is political. Before you disqualify yourself, think about why you hold the political beliefs that you do.

Suppose, for instance, that you object to war because it's a way for the rich to oppress the poor. This seems to be a political objection, but it may not be. Why do you think it's wrong for the rich to oppress the poor? What's wrong with injustice? The values that lead you to think that injustice is wrong may also qualify as the basis for a CO claim.

You may find that your beliefs have no religious, moral, or ethical basis at all. That's pretty unlikely, but if it's true, you're disqualified from CO status as the law now reads. But you can still file a CO claim. Your local board may think you do have a set of values which qualifies. And you'll at least be on record as to what you believe if you should decide to resist the draft.

Are You Sincere?

Many COs wonder not only how they can show their sincerity, but how their local boards can judge it.

If you present a CO claim that meets the legal standards the burden of proving that you don't qualify falls on your local board. They can't deny your claim merely because they suspect you are lying. "[D]oubt as to sincerity cannot be [based] on mere speculation." They will be looking for behavior that is inconsistent with your claim—for example, fighting if you claim to be nonviolent. They will look at your own story of how you became a CO. They should read your supporting letters, though local boards often don't. And, when you appear before them, they will be looking at you. If they find evidence that shows you are not telling the truth, they will deny your claim.

You can go a long way toward convincing your local

board by presenting a good CO claim. Chapter 18 will help you to do this.

"Late" Claims

Because you now can't file for CO status until you are called for induction, "late" filing (filing long after you've registered for the draft) shouldn't be as much of a problem as it used to be. You can't make a CO claim when you register, though you can follow the suggestions in Chapter 18 to get yourself on record. And it's a good idea to do so.

But even if you haven't put yourself on record before you file your formal CO claim, you local board can't deny your CO claim because it is "late." The regulations don't allow any choice. And even if you only decide at the last minute that you're a CO, your local board can't turn you down solely because you haven't been a CO all your life.

It's best, of course, to decide as soon as possible and start building a file as described in Chapter 18. But you must make your own decision in your own way. If it takes time for you to do so, that's all right.

Two Types of COs

The law divides conscientious objectors into two types:

✔ If you object to war but are willing to serve in the military without weapons, your local board should put you in class 1-A-0.

✔ If you object to war and also object to being in the military at all, your local board should put you in class 1-0.

Both 1-A-Os and 1-Os must object to all wars. Both

must be "religious" and sincere. If you ask for class 1-0, your local board can't give you l-A-0 as a "compromise" unless they believe you really don't object to being in the military. And if you ask for l-A-0, they must put you in class 1-0 if they find that you really are against being in the military.

The two kinds of objectors are very similar. The difference between them lies in where each draws his or her line. Most l-A-Os think it is not wrong for them to serve in the military as long as they personally do not kill. 1-Os disagree and think it is wrong to serve in the military at all.

Local boards are more likely to give l-A-0 status than 1-0 status because they know that l-A-Os become soldiers. But you shouldn't apply for l-A-0 status just because it's easier to get. If you feel you object to *any part* of being in the military, you should apply for 1-0 status.

How do you feel about wearing a military uniform? Following military orders? Being part of the military "chain of command"? If you object to any of these things, you should apply for 1-0 status.

Why Some People Object

This book can't tell you whether you should object to war, or why you might want to do so. That's for you to decide. But you might find it helpful to know about some of the reasons why others have applied for conscientious objector status. Here are a few.

✔ Some COs come from religious groups that have strong teachings against war, and decide to apply because they agree with the teachings of their religious group.

✔ Some COs come from religious groups which, while they don't oppose all wars, support COs. These people base their claims on their understanding of their religious group's teaching.

✔ Some COs come from no religious group, but consider themselves religious and base their claims on their own spiritual principles.

✔ Some COs come from no religious group, don't believe in a god or supreme being, and base their claims on moral principles.

✔ One CO in the Navy in 1993 based his claim on his belief that it is wrong to destroy the environment—and that all wars do just that.

✔ Some COs first decide to be COs because they oppose nuclear war and come to believe that any war could become a nuclear war.

All of these people, and many others with different convictions, can fit under the law's definition of a conscientious objector if their beliefs lead them to oppose all wars. For more on what this means, see the discussion in the next chapter.

Things to Think About

☞ What do you mean when you say "religion"? Do you agree with the law's definition?

☞ Do you think you might object to war in any form? What do these words mean to *you* (not to the law)?

Ideas for Papers

✍ Read and analyze the *Seeger* decision (you can get a copy from CCCO).

✍ Compare the *Seeger* and the *Welsh* decisions. How are they similar and how do they differ?

Chapter 4
Selective Objection

For many people considering conscientious objection, the hardest question is whether there are some wars in which they would be willing to fight. Most people are "selective objectors." That is, they would be willing to fight in some wars but would be conscientiously unwilling to participate in others. Even the toughest old general or admiral would admit under pressure that there are some wars their consciences would not permit them to fight—for example, if a President became senile and ordered an invasion of Canada. The key difference between a CO who qualifies under the law and a person who doesn't is that a legally-recognized CO won't take part in war no matter what its nature.

Selective and Non-Selective

The Selective Service law defines a CO as someone with a sincere objection to *participation in war in any form* or to the bearing of arms, by reason of religious training and belief. The key language here is "war in any form." If there is a war in which you know you would be willing to take part, then you are a selective objector. You do not qualify for legal recognition as a CO.

Historically the decision not to recognize selective

objection has been controversial. Supporters of selective objectors argue that people who sincerely object to participation in a war now being fought should be allowed to apply for CO status. The British had just such a policy during World War II. During the Vietnam War, the issue reached the Supreme Court in the case of *Gillette v. U.S.* The court decided in that case that selective objectors had no constitutional right to be exempted from military duty.

While this may seem a clear-cut rule, the line between a legally recognized CO and a selective objector is hazy. You may be willing to fight in some "wars," yet still qualify for legal CO status. Before you conclude that you're a selective objector, read the rest of this chapter. Maybe you do fit under the law after all.

✔ *Past and Future Wars:* In deciding whether you would fight in any wars, you don't have to put yourself in a time machine and decide for certain what you would have done many years ago or what you will do many years in the future. One question that is often asked of CO applicants is whether they would have fought in World War II. If your answer to this question is an absolute "yes," you cannot qualify for CO status unless you can show that the situations now and in World War II are completely different (see "Just and Unjust Wars," below, and Chapter 10 of this book).

On the other hand, if you are not certain what you would have done at that time because you can speak only for the person you are here and now, you can still qualify as a CO. That's also true for wars in the distant future. The *Gillette* case distinguished between people who knew that they would fight in some wars and people who couldn't swear that their beliefs would never change. Speaking of the second group, the Court said:

> Unwillingness to deny the possibility of a change of mind, in some hypothetical future circumstances, may be no more than humble good sense, casting no doubt on the claimant's present sincerity of belief.

So if you don't know what you would do in the future, you may still qualify as a conscientious objector.

✔ *Other Hypothetical Wars:* Would you fight if the world were invaded by forces of evil from outer space? Your local board, your friends, or your neighbors might ask you this, but you don't need to have an answer. You don't have to know what you would do in wars you think are impossible—or in wars you would never be called upon to serve in. If you don't have an answer, you can say so. That's true also for realistic wars. For instance, you can't know what you would think if you were living in South Africa, so you can't know whether you would fight in a war there. If somebody asks you, it's all right to say you don't know. The real issue is whether you would take part in any war you could actually be called upon to fight.

Just and Unjust Wars

Many religious traditions distinguish between just and unjust wars. Those who follow a "just war" theory—either from their religious tradition or as a result of their own thinking—believe they should fight only in wars which meet their definition of a just war. Most just war thinking is designed to *prevent* wars, not to help governments to rationalize them, but phrases like "just war" and "just cause" are often misused. (The U.S. invasion of Panama in 1989 was actually called "Operation Just Cause.") Just war theories also often try to help soldiers decide between right and wrong actions once war has started—for example, by forbidding deliberate killing of civilians.

In the West, the Christian just war theory, which goes back to St. Augustine in the 4th Century A.D., is the best-known. Theologians do not agree on exactly what the standards for a just war may be, or how many of them there are. The most common "just war" standards, however, are the eight below. It may be helpful to see how they apply to some recent wars.

✔ War must be the last resort after all other possible solutions have been tried and failed.

✔ The reason for the war must be to redress rights actually violated or to defend against unjust demands backed by force.

✔ The war must be openly and legally declared by a lawful government.

✔ There must be a reasonable chance of winning.

✔ Soldiers must try to distinguish between armies and civilians and never kill civilians on purpose.

✔ The means used in fighting the war must be "proportionate" to the end sought. The good to be done by the war must outweigh the evil which the war would do.

✔ The winner must never require the utter humiliation of the loser.

Vietnam and the Gulf War

The Vietnam War (1954-1975) violated at least six of these standards. It wasn't a last resort. The rights of the U.S. hadn't been violated, and the U.S. hadn't been attacked. The war was undeclared. Far from there being a chance of victory, no one in the government even knew what "victory" meant. The means—like dropping millions of tons of bombs on North Vietnam—were out of proportion to whatever end the war sought (except the total destruction of Vietnam). U.S. soldiers, under orders, killed thousands of civilians in "search-and-destroy" missions and similar operations. Nobody will ever know, of course, whether the U.S. wanted to humiliate the Vietnamese.

The Persian Gulf War (1991) was widely thought to be a just war because the Allies were fighting to repel Iraq's illegal invasion of Kuwait. You'll have to decide for yourself whether it met the just war standards, but there's a good argument that it didn't meet some of the eight standards above. It wasn't a last resort, for example. Right up to the start of the air war, the Allies could have decided to rely on economic sanctions against Iraq rather than make war. And it's not clear that the destruction caused by the war was "proportional" to the end sought. Over 100,000 Iraqis, mostly civilians, were killed in the air war, and according to a United Nations evaluation, the bombing reduced Iraq to near "stone age" conditions in some places.

Working Through Your Beliefs

If you oppose the use of force at all times, the question of whether you're a CO or a selective objector is simple because all wars involve the use of force. But if you're not sure where you draw the line, this is a hard question. After you consider the basic legal distinction and exceptions discussed above, consider how your own beliefs might fit in. Remember that if there is a war you would fight in, it must be a war you think might realistically happen, and one you might be asked to take part in. If it isn't, your willingness to fight may not disqualify you from legal CO status.

If you're not sure what you would do if the country were attacked, consider whether you believe any country would attack the United States and what such an attack would be like. Do you think someone would attack the U.S. without using nuclear missiles? How likely do you think such an attack really is? And remember that there are many things you could do to support your family, community, and nation if the country were attacked, short of joining the military.

Are You a Conscientious Objector?

If you don't know whether you qualify but definitely oppose all the wars you can think of, you may well qualify for CO status. Try writing down you beliefs to clarify them in your own mind. Since the differences between selective objection and legal conscientious objection aren't always clear, it's possible that you will find that you qualify.

Even if you're sure you are a selective objector, there are good reasons for thinking about what you believe—and for getting ready to make a CO application, just in case the draft is revived. First, if you do apply, you give yourself a chance to get CO status should your local board see your claim as applying to all wars.

Second, by applying and going through the CO processing, you will both document your position and make it clear to the government that you are taking all possible legal steps. While this may not result in your recognition as a CO, it might provide a defense in court or lead to a lighter sentence if you find that you have to refuse induction.

Third and finally, many people continue to feel that the United States laws should recognize selective objectors. By applying for CO status and sending copies of your application to your religious group (if you have one) and to your Congress members, you can help work toward recognition of selective objectors in the United States at some time in the future.

Things to Think About

☞ If you're a member of a church, what is your church's teaching about war? Does your church accept a form of "just war" theory? Does it support conscientious objectors? Do you agree with its position?

☞ Do you think any war can meet the "just war" standards?

Ideas for Papers

✍ Explain the "just war" theory and show how it applies to an a actual war. Was the war "just" or "unjust" according to the theory.

✍ Talk to a person who opposed the Vietnam War or the Gulf War and write a description and analysis of the conversation.

Part III

Thinking About War

Chapter 5
You and the Military

The United States military is the most powerful on earth. Even after proposed cutbacks, it will have 1.4 million active-duty soldiers and nearly 8 million Reservists. Its weapons range from rifles and tanks to nerve gas and guided missiles. It has bases, with large numbers of troops, in Europe and Asia. Its nuclear submarines, each armed with missiles than can destroy many cities, cruise the oceans at all times. If it released all of its nuclear weapons, it could destroy the entire human race twelve times over—or perhaps more.

To maintain its troop strength, the military must recruit 250,000 or more new soldiers each year. From 1948 through 1972, it used a combination of the draft and voluntary recruitment. Since 1972, it has recruited without the draft. But the draft remains on "standby" and could again become part of the recruitment system. (For more on this, see Appendix 3 of this book.)

The Uses of the Military

Following World War II, the name of the War Department was changed to "Defense Department." Despite this name change, very little of the Defense budget actually goes for the defense of the United States. Much is spent on troops stationed around the world, on waste, and on weapons systems that have little or no military value.

Defending the U.S.

From a military point of view, the United States could be defended by a much smaller Army, Navy, and Air Force than it now has. It has northern and southern borders with friendly countries, and those borders have not been patrolled by the military for over a hundred years. On the east and west, it is bordered by oceans. An attack over water on the continental U.S., as you'll see in Chapter 11, would be so difficult that no general would try it. And to destroy almost any enemy, the U.S. would need to use only a small part of its nuclear arsenal.

Why, then, is the U.S. military as large as it is? The answer lies partly in American politics, where candidates can win votes by being for a "strong defense." It also lies partly in the doctrine of "deterrence," which says that the way to prevent an attack is to have so many weapons that your opponent will think the attack won't be worth the cost. For more on "deterrence," see Chapter 8.

But politics and "deterrence" alone don't explain why this country has such a large military. Since World War II ended, this country has used military force or the threat of military force over 200 times. What was this supposed to do?

Geopolitics and Natural Resources

One reason why the U.S. keeps so many troops when there is no war is "geopolitics." This is the contest among the countries of the world for power and influence. Between 1948 and 1990, the U.S. and the former Soviet Union were the two most powerful countries in the world. The two "superpowers" engaged in a "Cold War" in which each tried to gain power and influence to counter the other. During the Cold War, the U.S. government justified almost all of its military decisions by citing the threat of Communism, and the Soviet government said that it was fighting capitalism. In practice, both supported their allies with weapons, economic aid, military advice, and sometimes troops— very much as great powers have always done. The end of the Cold War in 1990 did not mean the end of "geopolitics."

Today, like many other countries, the U.S. tries to gain influence in other countries, or power over them, using economic aid, military aid, persuasion—and military force. If, for instance, Washington thinks that a friendly government is going to be overthrown, it may send military aid or even troops to help that government. It may even, as the U.S. did in Vietnam, install a government of its own choice to replace the one that is weak. "Geopolitics" often leads to military intervention. During the Cold War, the U.S. fought wars of intervention in Korea, the Dominican Republic, Vietnam, Grenada, and Panama—among other places. In 1990, U.S. forces intervened in the Persian Gulf; the official reason for this war was protecting world oil supplies. The U.S. also sent troops to Somalia in 1992. For more discussion of these and other interventions, see "New Roles for the Military," below.

But "geopolitics" doesn't always lead to a shooting

war. Between World War II and the end of the Cold War in 1990, the U.S. signed treaties agreeing that it would defend many countries. The most famous of these is the North Atlantic Treaty Organization, or NATO, which was supposed to prevent the Soviet Union from conquering Europe. The Soviet Union, in its turn, signed a treaty, called the Warsaw Pact, with the Communist governments of Eastern Europe. One purpose of the Warsaw Pact was to "balance" NATO—to keep NATO from conquering Eastern Europe. NATO also sought to balance the Warsaw Pact. Each side did this by deploying troops and weapons systems. And when one side deployed a new system, the other was almost sure to follow suit. This was geopolitics without a shot fired. You'll have to decide for yourself whether it made war more or less likely.

Outside Europe, the U.S., and other countries compete in the Third World, not just for influence, but for natural resources. You've heard a great deal about the Middle East and oil, but the Third World provides other resources as well. Many important metals, like chromium, are no longer found in the U.S. U.S. troops are sometimes used to protect U.S. interests in countries that have natural resources. This doesn't always mean sending ground troops. It could mean sending an aircraft carrier to a region to restore stability.

At the same time, many Third World countries are saying that they have the right to decide for themselves what they will do with their natural resources. Unpopular governments are often overthrown by guerrilla movements. Many of these governments were friendly to the U.S. This could lead to more wars of intervention.

It could change the balance of power in the world. Or it could do both.

Jobs and Inertia

When the Warsaw Pact disbanded in 1990, NATO might also have disbanded, but it did not. When this book went to press, it was still seeking a mission. This shows another reason for our large military: inertia. Our thinking about the military doesn't usually change as fast as the times.

Another reason why many people support a large military is economics. Having a defense plant or a military base in a community can mean many additional civilian jobs. When the military closed many of its bases in the early 1990s, Congress members from districts with military bases fought to preserve the bases in their districts—not just because of "national security," but because of the jobs that would be lost if the base closed.

Maintaining all these uses of the military takes millions of troops, billions of dollars worth of weapons, and hundreds of billions of dollars in tax money each year.

New Roles for the Military

With the end of the Cold War in 1990, the U.S. military had lost its major purpose—countering the Soviet military. Military and civilian strategists spent a lot of time discussing what the military's new job would be. While the debate went on, the U.S. fought a war in the Persian Gulf, sent troops to Somalia, and tried to persuade its European allies to intervene in the civil war in Bosnia-Herzegovina. The government justified each of these interventions (or proposed interventions) by talking about new roles for the military. Some strategists suggested still other uses for the military. What were these suggestions? What do they mean for the future? Here are some of them and some thoughts about each.

The "War on Drugs"

During the late 1980s and early 1990s, the U.S. sent troops to Colombia to support local troops in their war against the Colombian drug cartels. (Many "drug lords," in Colombia and in other places such as Southeast Asia, have private armies that are organized like regular or guerrilla military forces.) The U.S. Coast Guard has also spent the majority of its budget trying to find and detain ships carrying drugs.

These military actions were supposed to stop illegal drugs from entering the U.S., either by cutting them off at the source or by stopping them at the border. Most experts think the "war on drugs" failed, and most military commanders thought it was a bad use of their troops.

International Police Force

During and after the Persian Gulf War (1991), President Bush talked about a "New World Order," in which the international community would punish aggressors and keep the peace. Officially, the war against Iraq was a United Nations effort; unofficially, the major forces were those of the United States, and without U.S. initiative there would have been no war.

The Gulf War was not the first United Nations "police action." Following North Korea's invasion of the south in 1950, President Truman sought U.N. approval for joint military action to defeat the invasion. As in the Persian Gulf, however, most of the troops were from the

U.S., and the war probably would not have happened without U.S. initiative.

Should the United States try to police the world? What does it mean to set up an international police force? Why did we "police" Iraq in 1990 and not Serbia (which invaded other countries and supported atrocities in Bosnia) in 1992? These are questions that many people, not just conscientious objectors, find troubling.

Peacekeeping

In Korea and Iraq, U.S. and Allied forces fought just as they would have in any other war. They not only defended themselves, but sought out and attacked opposing armies. "Peacekeeping" forces, whether commanded by the United Nations or by one country, are supposed to be different from a regular army. They are supposed to go into a country where there has been a war to help maintain a cease-fire or treaty which both sides have agreed to. They are also supposed to fight only to defend themselves.

In practice, peacekeeping forces often don't achieve very much. In Bosnia-Herzegovina in 1992-1993, there were many cease-fires, but none of them lasted longer than two or three days. UN peacekeepers in the Middle East did not prevent the Israeli invasion of Lebanon in 1982.

On the other hand, peacekeeping forces in Cambodia in the early 1990s did help to arrange national elections which in turn helped to move a bloody civil war toward a peaceful settlement. So peacekeeping forces can be helpful if used wisely.

What do you think about peacekeeping forces? Do

you think that military forces can really act as peace-keepers? What does it mean to maintain the peace? These are difficult questions for anyone, not just for conscientious objectors.

"Humanitarian Intervention"

Toward the end of 1992, President Bush ordered 25,000 U.S. troops to go to Somalia, where many people were starving. The military's mission was to safeguard food shipments and restore order, which had broken down because of a civil war. In the spring of 1993, most of the U.S. troops left, to be replaced by UN troops.

The intervention in Somalia was supposed to be an entirely new kind of military operation—"humanitarian intervention." By protecting food shipments, it was supposed to help feed the starving, and by restoring order it was supposed to help the Somalis rebuild their country so that large-scale hunger wouldn't happen again.

In the late spring of 1993, the United Nations forces, including the remaining U.S. forces, began an offensive against one of the factions in the civil war. This action, which was like any other military attack, raised the question whether there was such a thing as "humanitarian intervention" by military forces. Critics of the action in Somalia, including some aid groups with workers there, also argued that the troops may have done more harm than good—for instance, that they hadn't really helped the Somalis to rebuild their agriculture and food distribution systems.

Do you think military forces can be used for humanitarian purposes? In a world with many wars and much suffering, this is a question everyone will have to face.

Recruiting the Military

Tens of thousands of troops leave the military each year. Some leave because their time is up. Others get early discharges because they are not doing well in the military, because of family problems, or for other reasons. To replace those who leave, the military recruits 250,000 or more new troops each year.

Military recruitment today relies on a combination of high unemployment among young people, advertising campaigns, and promises of education and job training. Pentagon figures show that as unemployment among young people rises, military recruitment also goes up. The military spends tens of millions of dollars on advertising each year. And recruiters persuade many people to come into the military by telling them about special programs like electronics school and promising them education and training in a field they choose.

For many recruits, the promise of education and training quickly turns to disappointment. Military enlistment agreements allow the military to keep a recruit even when the military doesn't fulfill its promises. And the needs of the military are more important to military planners than providing education for a new recruit. A recruit who was promised training in auto mechanics may get the training he or she was promised—and then be assigned to work in artillery.

In addition, much military training teaches skills that are of no use in civilian life. A person experienced in artillery, for instance, isn't likely to find civilian work in that field. Artillery is used only in the military.

Minority soldiers and women often find that they're no more equal in the military than they would be in civilian life—sometimes less. In the military as a whole, African-Americans are more than 10% of enlisted people; a far smaller percentage of officers are African-American. And women often end up stuck in traditional "women's jobs," like typing.

It's not surprising that many people want to leave the military early or don't want to reenlist when their hitches are up. For more on military recruitment, see Chapter 13.

Your Decision

You have to make a lot of decisions when you reach military age. Among those decisions is whether you can be part of war.

If you're a man subject to draft registration, you face an additional choice: What will you do about draft registration? Many people are against the standby draft and refuse to go along with it. These resisters often object not only to war, but to the idea of conscription itself. In addition to making war easier and more deadly, they say, the draft interferes with people's lives and their rights.

You'll have to decide for yourself whether you agree with this—and whether you'll go along with draft registration if you should face it. Before you can decide this, though, you need to think about war, where you stand on it, and what this means for your life. That's what most of this book is about.

Things to Think About

☞ What do you think is the most important reason why

the U.S. has such a large military?

☞ Why do you think the U.S. needs so many natural resources from other countries?

☞ Do you support the idea of "humanitarian intervention"? How would you help suffering people in war-torn countries?

☞ Do you think there should be an international police force? What do you think it should do?

☞ How do you think the U.S. can deal with the problem of drugs?

☞ Are war and the military different for African-Americans? For Latinos? For women? If you think they are different for each of these groups, think about how and why.

Ideas for Papers

✍ Somalia during the Cold War—did the U.S. and the Soviet Union compete there? If they did, why?

✍ Did the Persian Gulf War help preserve Western oil supplies? Why or why not?

✍ What is the purpose of Selective Service registration? Does it fulfill its purpose? Why or why not?

Chapter 6
Some Thoughts on War

Historians, politicians, sociologists, psychologists, anthropologists, military officers, pacifists, and other citizens have studied war almost since the beginning of civilization. They have written hundreds of books, articles, and reports of studies. They have argued for and against war, traced it to different causes, and suggested many different ways to end it.

Yet few people even agree on what war is. Was the Cold War a war? Does there have to be a declaration of war? If so, what was Vietnam, where there was no declaration? What was Korea, which was called a "police action"? Is guerrilla warfare really war, or do we need a new name for it? What about terrorism?

The courts haven't really ruled on what war means as a matter of law. Among the cases on conscientious objection are many on force and violence which distinguish the use of force from war. But there is no case which *defines* war. A state court in Virginia ruled in the late 1960s that, for life insurance purposes, the Vietnam conflict was a war. Even that court, though, didn't try to define war.

Historians don't even always agree on when wars begin. World War I began officially on a known and agreed date (August 4, 1914). But some historians think that World War II began when the Japanese invaded Manchuria in 1932. Others think it began with Hitler's invasion of Poland in 1939. Still others think that the Far East wars of 1932-1941 and the European war of 1939-1941 were separate wars, and that the World War didn't begin until the Japanese bombed Pearl Harbor in 1941.

A Definition of War

This chapter won't try to resolve these disputes. Instead, it will define war as armed conflict between two or more countries or between rival military forces within one country. This means that the Battle of Waterloo was part of a war, as were the Battle of Verdun in 1916 and the Siege of Dien Bien Phu in 1954. Guerrilla warfare comes under this definition. World Wars I and II, Korea, Vietnam, and Afghanistan, among others, are wars by this definition.

In order for war to be taking place, there needn't be a declaration of war. A declaration of war is a diplomatic device, and it has legal effects both internationally and within the country that has declared war. (For instance, parts of the U.S. draft law don't apply after a declaration of war.) But few wars today are formally declared. Vietnam was not. Afghanistan was not. The Iran-Iraq war of the early 1980s was not. In the Persian Gulf War of 1991, Congress authorized the President to use force, but it never formally declared war on Iraq. And so on.

The Cold War wasn't a war by this chapter's definition. It was "geopolitics," as discussed in Chapter 5. The military forces of the U.S. and the Soviet Union competed all the time for better strategic position. They did this by buying new weapons, moving their forces around, preparing strategic plans, and by actual shows of force like sending an aircraft carrier to a trouble spot. But there was no direct armed conflict between the two countries. There was only the threat of war—and of total destruction, as you'll see in Chapter 8.

War and the Arms Race

Many historians believe that arms races in themselves don't cause wars. This may surprise you. Common sense tells you that when two countries mistrust each other and arm against each other, they're more likely to fight.

But the argument isn't as weak as it sounds. The causes of any particular war are many, and it's hard to know which is most important. And the causes of war itself—the explanation of why people fight—may not even include the arms race. It may be that people make weapons because they're willing to fight—not that people are willing to fight because they make weapons.

Still, arms races increase world tensions. This could make war more likely. And by increasing the firepower on both sides, an arms race makes a war, if it comes, larger and more terrible. But the relationship between war and the arms race is pretty complex.

There's a good argument, for instance, that war causes the arms race, not the reverse. Military planners base much of their thinking on what wars they believe are likely. The arms race may be called "defense" or "a necessary response to imperialist aggression, " or whatever. In fact, it is a preparation for war. Types of weapons, size of armies, and placement of troops are determined mainly by plans for future wars.

An example of this is U.S. war plans. In the early 1960s, Pentagon planners tried to be prepared for two wars—one in Europe and one in another part of the world. Then, under the Nixon administration, they were directed to plan for 1 1/2 wars—a large one in Europe and a small one somewhere else. In the 1980s they prepared for a large war in Europe and a "crisis" in another part of the world. Each of these predictions means a different size army, different weapons, and different strategies. And the U.S. is armed, as most other nations are, because it accepts war as one way of settling international disputes or gaining power.

Whether war causes the arms race, or the arms race causes war, there's no doubt that, when the shooting starts, the arms race speeds up. Both sides arm themselves as heavily as they can, and both try to develop new weapons quickly, before their opponents do.

Between 1870 and 1914, for instance, there was no war in Europe. Few new weapons were developed. During World War I, however, literally hundreds of new weapons were made and tried. Many are now standard in warfare: the tank, the flamethrower, the airplane, aerial bombing, and the trench mortar, among others. Others are against the "laws of war," but could still be used in a future war. Poison gas was outlawed right after the 1914-1918 war, but many countries have huge stocks of gas like that used in World War I, and worse gas, such as the U.S. military's nerve gas.

Structure of the Military

A modern army fights what is called "drilled warfare." This name comes from the use of drill in training troops. The basic structure of Western-style armies hasn't changed much since Roman times. At the top of the army is a supreme commander who sets overall strategy. Below the commander is a "chain of command," made up of lower-ranking officers.

The military is built up from small units, each under the command of a low-ranking officer (like a lieutenant) or a high-ranking enlisted person (like a sergeant). Several of these small units make up a larger unit, and several of these larger units make up a still larger unit, and so on up the chain of command.

The reason for all this dividing up is to make military units interchangeable, like machine parts. In combat, a soldier may be killed or wounded. A unit may have too many killed and wounded and become "exhausted." Or the strain of fighting may make it less "combat-effective." One unit must be able to replace another that can no longer fight. And one soldier must be able to replace another who is killed, wounded, or battle-weary. So the military is divided into standard parts. Military jobs are standard, so that anybody can learn them.

Although a modern army may draw its officers from all walks of life, the division between officers (higher-ranking soldiers who command and plan strategy) and enlisted persons (lower-ranking soldiers under the command of officers) goes back to early armies in which the lower-ranking soldiers were drawn from the lower ranks of society and the officers were drawn from the nobility. Many military customs like separate clubs for officers also have their roots in earlier armies. This makes the command structure into a kind of class structure.

The military hierarchy makes it very difficult for a

low-ranking soldier to challenge unreasonable orders or abuses of power. And it means that in many cases enlisted soldiers run greater risks than officers. But this isn't always so. In Vietnam, for instance, 2nd Lieutenants commanding combat units had a very high casualty rate. And in the World War I British army, an officer in the front lines had an average life expectancy of six weeks; an enlisted man might expect to live for ten weeks.

The military structure is supposed to help officers in planning operations. Instead of moving one soldier here and another there, strategists can move entire units. In most armies, the local commander can choose tactics that suit conditions like weather, terrain, etc. On paper, this makes for efficient operations. It doesn't, of course, always work that way in practice. Some of the reasons why this happens will be found under "Combat," below.

The Weapons of War

Throughout history, military forces have used whatever weapons they had, and they have tried to develop new weapons to gain an advantage over their opponents. The result, today, is that armies have a choice of thousands of different weapons and tactics. Most modern weapons are designed to destroy and kill people at a distance. Examples would be artillery, guided missiles, and the rifle. Some weapons kill automatically, without a human being to fire them.

During the Indochina War, for instance, American forces used electronic weapons (like very sophisticated minefields) which would fire if anyone crossed certain parts of the jungle. And some weapons, called "smart" weapons, track their targets using built-in controls like heat-seeking devices and computers. Many "smart" weapons have—at least in theory—a 90% chance of hitting their targets.

Not all modern weapons are designed merely to kill. Anti-personnel weapons, as military planners call them, are designed to disable and maim as well. One weapon used during the Vietnam War sprayed plastic pellets when it exploded. These transparent bullets would wound anyone within range, and they would be very difficult to remove. The idea was to tie up enemy hospitals with long and complicated surgery.

Weapons like napalm (a compound which burns and sticks to human flesh), the automatic battlefield, and anti-personnel explosives do not distinguish between enemy soldiers and civilians. Neither do bombs dropped from airplanes. That is why, in many modern wars, there are far more civilian than military casualties. The last major war where this was not true, in fact, was World War I.

Some people think that weapons like these—and others which haven't yet been used, like nerve gas — have made even modern "conventional" (non-nuclear) war unjustified. Many who hold these views might have fought in past wars, but would not fight today. Yet even in past wars, as far back as ancient times, technology was used for terrible destruction. Towns were burned using weapons similar to napalm. Wells were poisoned. Some ancient armies even used a kind of poison gas.

Has anything really changed? You'll have to decide this question for yourself. In any case, there's no doubt that modern war is far more destructive than the wars of, say, the 1700s. This is because of modern weapons, but it is also because tactics have changed and become more ruthless. For more on this, see Chapter 7 of this book.

The Laws of War

Even among people who thought some wars were justified, there have been many attempts to control the destruction which war causes. The "laws of war" cover everything from treatment of wounded and prisoners to which weapons can lawfully be used. The "laws of war," however, aren't quite like the laws which you follow every day—for example, traffic laws or laws against robbery. They are based on agreements among the nations of the world, called "conventions," and on precedents like the Nuremberg War Crimes Trials. There isn't any real way to enforce them, and there's no court that can order a country, say, to stop using poison gas.

This means that countries at war don't always follow the laws of war. And sometimes it means that the laws of war don't make a great deal of sense. For instance, an international convention outlaws the use of poison gas. No convention outlaws the machine gun. Yet the machine gun has been used far more than poison has, and it has killed far more people.

If you're a conscientious objector, you probably think that war itself is so evil that no "laws of war" can make it better. In many ways that's true. But without the "laws of war," prisoners might still be slaughtered, as they were in ancient wars. There might be no Red Cross to help the wounded. And nations which have, say, nerve gas might be quicker to use it.

For people in the military, the "laws of war" can be very important. A U.S. military member has a legal right to refuse an order that violates international conventions. Most soldiers don't do this because they don't know they can or because they're afraid of what might happen to them. But if you decide to go into the military and find that you're given orders against your conscience, you may be able to refuse the orders. You shouldn't, of course, refuse any order until you've talked with CCCO or a military counselor.

Combat

The reason for nearly everything that armies do — from training to medical services to the design of boots— is combat. If an army cannot fight when the shooting starts, it will fail in its main mission

This seems clear enough. And it seems clear enough what combat is. It is actual armed conflict. An army's object in combat is to kill, wound, or capture the other side's soldiers and take over the other side's territory and positions without losing more of its own soldiers than it has to. Military thinkers argue about whether a winning army must destroy the other army, convince the other side's generals that they can't win, or destroy the other side's ability to fight by destroying factories and killing civilians. In modern total war, this kind of argument means less than it once did. Modern armies try to do all three.

Armies today fight, in many ways, as they have for centuries. They follow a strategy (overall plan) using tactics (methods of fighting) based on conditions where they are fighting and the weapons they are using. Modern armies are said to fight in three "dimensions:" land, sea, and air. On land, they use artillery to shock and kill their opponents from a distance. They use tanks to move into good positions more quickly than their opponents and to destroy communications and defenses. They use infantry (foot soldiers) to "secure" positions and go places where tanks can't. Airplanes attack the other side's soldiers or cities. Ships can cut off the other side's supplies or attack the other army from a distance (for instance, by shelling a beach).

The "art of war" has become very complex and destructive. But the aim of combat hasn't changed very much over the years. Combat consists of killing and destroying according to a plan, and avoiding being killed and destroyed at the same time. The army with the best plan often wins—but not always.

Combat is unpredictable. People and units aren't really interchangeable. Combat is noisy, deadly, dirty, and frightening. No matter how well-trained a soldier is, he or she may break under the strain. Or something may go wrong—a tank may fail to start, or soldiers may be killed by their own side's fire. Or even a well-trained soldier may go berserk and kill anyone in sight.

This doesn't happen often because soldiers usually follow orders. In fact, you could say that, while combat is violent, soldiers, for the most part, are not. They're ordinary people in a terrible situation. It's important to remember this as you're thinking about war. Combat soldiers are probably about your age. Before they were trained to fight, they were very much like you. They still are. Military training, where actions like firing a gun are repeated until they become automatic, makes them able to kill. And in combat, they do things which they wouldn't do on the street.

Combat soldiers are following orders. They do this because they're afraid of punishment and humiliation in front of their fellow soldiers. They do it because it's automatic after their training. And they do it because combat is one of the most frightening situations a person can be in. Most people will defend themselves if they're threatened. That's even more true when you've gone through military training.

But a soldier's training doesn't make him or her inhuman. One of the worst costs of war is the thousands of soldiers who have been in combat and survived—and now have to live with the memory of what they saw and what they were forced to do. Many find it very hard, indeed.

War and the Environment

War destroys not only people and property, but the environment as well. It's easy to see its direct effects. Cities where combat has taken place are blasted to ruins. Trees become stumps without leaves, branches, or identity. Fields change from green to brown—from living places to dead ones.

With time, most areas where combat has taken place return to normal—but not entirely. Some World War I battlefields still hold unexploded shells, and the forests in the hills surrounding Verdun, where one of the most terrible battles in history took place, have never entirely regrown.

Modern military technology has not only increased

the damage that armies can do; it has added long-term damage to short-term destruction. The U.S. forces in Vietnam, for example, tried to "defoliate" the jungles using a weed-killer called Agent Orange. Parts of Vietnam remain lifeless even twenty years after the war because of "defoliation," and people, including Vietnam veterans, who were exposed to Agent Orange are still feeling its medical effects.

As modern weapons increase in their power, it is likely that warfare will become even more dangerous to the environment. But the direct effects of war on the environment are not the only ones. War also affects the environment indirectly, by using scarce resources. The making of modern weapons, particularly nuclear weapons, can and does pollute the environment so badly that its long-term effects are only now beginning to be understood.

In recent years, some COs have submitted claims which cited war's destruction of the environment as one reason for opposing it. Even people who don't object to war are troubled by the way that war affects the environment, both in combat and in peacetime. What do you think?

Militarism

One side-effect of war and preparing for war is militarism. Sidney B. Fay, a well-known expert on the origins of World War I, gave two definitions of militarism: "First, the dangerous and burdensome mechanism of great standing armies and large navies, with the attendant evils of espionage, suspicion, fear, and hatred. Second, the existence of a powerful class of military and naval officers ... who tend to dominate, especially at a time of political crisis, over the civilian authorities." Another definition says that militarism is the love of military things like uniforms, weapons, and parades—for themselves. A fourth says that militarism is the belief that military force can solve all or most of the problems which a nation has in its foreign policy.

As you can imagine, militarism can often be dangerous. Many people in the U.S., for instance, believe that the solution to shortages of oil and raw materials is to increase U.S. military strength. Whether or not this is true, it probably increases the chances of war. So does the belief that military values are "strong," and therefore good, and peaceful values are "weak," and therefore bad.

The Causes of War

Thinkers over the centuries have argued about the cause of war. Some anthropologists believe that humans have a "killer instinct" which leads them to make war. Marxists and many others hold that war is caused by a need for capitalist countries to expand their markets. Others think that war is caused by misunderstandings that result because the people on both sides don't know each other well enough. Still others argue that wars happen because each nation acts like a law unto itself in foreign affairs.

All of these ideas have some basis, and all have some flaws. The "killer instinct," for instance, hasn't been proved. In fact, much of the evidence is the other way. And even if there were a "killer instinct," that wouldn't explain how a particular war, like World War II, began.

Sidney B. Fay said that we must separate the immediate causes of war from its underlying causes. This is a good place to begin in trying to understand the causes of war. When you read about a war in history, you can learn much by trying to see how that particular war got started. Was it because of blunders by diplomats? Attacks by one nation on another? Or what?

At the same time, this won't tell you much about why there are wars at all. And that's an important —and much harder—question. You can study it for years and still not really know. But you can learn a lot by trying, if you're interested.

One thing is clear. Whatever causes war, there wouldn't be any wars at all if people refused to fight. And after all is said and done, that's the main issue for you: Will you fight or not? You can decide this without knowing the causes of any war. You're the only expert on this question.

Things to Think About

☞ What is your definition of war?

☞ Do you think arms races are dangerous? Why or why not?

☞ Do you support idea of having laws of war? Why or why not?

☞ Why do you think soldiers fight instead of running away or hiding from combat? What do you think you would do?

☞ Do you think people are "naturally warlike"? If so, how does this explain the many wars in history? If not, how do you explain the many wars in history?

Ideas for Papers

✍ Write a brief history of how one weapon—for

instance, the rifle—has changed over the years and how that has changed warfare.

✍ Compare warfare before and after the invention of gunpowder.

✍ Write a paper analyzing the effect of one war, such as the Vietnam War, on the environment.

✍ Interview a combat veteran and analyze your impressions of the interview.

Chapter 7
Conventional and Unconventional Wars

In 1815, the Duke of Wellington's forces defeated those of Napoleon at the Battle of Waterloo. The battlefield was so small that Wellington personally visited most parts of it while the battle was taking place. Local farmers actually watched the fighting from a hill nearby. The battle ended after one day.

It is difficult to imagine a similar battle today. Modern weapons are so much more destructive than those used in 1815 that civilians near the combat zone would not stay to watch but, if they could, flee for their lives. A modern "battlefield" can include entire countries. Fighting can go on for weeks or even months.

Modern war is different from older wars. This chapter discusses how it differs from earlier wars, when the modern era in warfare began, and some issues for you to think about as you decide whether to be a conscientious objector. It is only an introduction. If you want to learn more, read some of the books recommended under "Further Reading" at the end of this book.

When Did Modern War Begin?

Historians do not agree on when war began to be "modern." Many date the modern era in warfare to the

American Civil War (1861-1865), but, though that war was like today's wars in many ways, it did not include air war (except for observation balloons), and modern armored war had not yet been invented. World War I (1914-1918) led to the invention of many modern weapons and tactics, but missiles and guidance systems, which were an important part of the Persian Gulf War (1991), did not exist. Missiles were first used late in World War II (1939-1945), and modern guidance systems were developed long after the end of that war.

What all this shows is that war has changed over the years. To understand modern war and why it is so devastating, you have to look at how it evolved as well as how armies fight today. For simplicity, this chapter will assume that modern war began to develop during the Civil War.

How Is Modern War Different?

Modern armies differ from older armies in six major ways:

Size: Modern armies are usually larger than pre-Civil War armies. Even after cutbacks, for example, the U.S. active military will have 1.4 million troops—a far larger force than most pre-Civil War armies—*in peacetime.* In wartime, the U.S. military might grow to eight or ten million.

Mechanization: At Waterloo, infantry on both sides fought with single-shot muskets. The Civil War saw the introduction of the first machine gun. Though unreliable and difficult to use, the Gatling Gun changed warfare forever because it was a *machine* which killed impersonally. By World War I, the machine gun had become the most deadly of all infantry weapons.

Firepower: Modern weapons are more destructive than those of earlier eras. The armies at Waterloo, for example, had artillery but not explosive shells. Modern shells and missiles carry deadly explosive charges, including smaller "bomblets" or mines which spread over a large area and then explode, causing far more damage than a single explosion.

Mobility: Tanks and troop transporters, helicopters, strike aircraft, and transportation aircraft allow modern armies to fight and cause destruction over very wide areas—including entire countries.

Accuracy of Weapons: During the Persian Gulf War, television audiences in the U.S. saw film of missiles which could enter a building, locate an exact target, and hit it. These "smart" weapons, or precision-guided munitions, were supposed to cut down on civilian casualties. The television images were misleading because less than ten percent of U.S. weapons in the Gulf air war were "smart," and many of these hit the wrong targets. Modern weapons, however, are usually more accurate and reliable than weapons in older wars. This, combined with their increased explosive power, can only increase the numbers of dead and wounded. The Gulf air war killed over 100,000 Iraqis, many of them civilians, in less than a month.

Tactics: Modern warfare includes many tactics which are violations of international law or are questionable on moral grounds. See the discussions under "Total War" and "Battlefield Tactics," below.

Total War

Modern war is often called "total war." Total war is often thought to be new in this century, but in many ways it isn't. Ancient wars, for instance, were often total in the sense that the loser's cities and crops were destroyed, the men slaughtered, and the women and children taken captive.

But today's total war is so different from past wars that it is a new development. Before the mid-19th Century, armies were small, and most wars were fought on battlefields away from the civilian population. A country that went to war didn't put all its industry to work making war supplies and ammunition, as happens today. There was no such thing as bombing of cities, though cities were often besieged and even destroyed.

All this began to change with the Civil War. In that war, armies—and casualties—were huge by the standards of past wars. The railroad made troop movements easier and more rapid than they had ever been before. The telegraph made for fast communication. Even the weapons used were rifles that shot modern-style bullets, rather than muskets which shot lead balls as in earlier wars.

Most important, the Civil War saw the first use of a deliberate attack against the enemy's population rather than the enemy's army. For many people, this is what makes modern war different from past wars. Gen. William Tecumseh Sherman of the Union Army believed that the best way to defeat the Confederacy was to destroy its economy and its "will to fight." His troops first occupied and destroyed Atlanta—then, as now, a major trade center. They then marched in a line fifty miles wide from Atlanta to the Georgia coast, burning crops, killing those who resisted them, and destroying property as they went. This "March to the Sea" split the Confederacy and ruined its economy, just as Sherman had predicted. It was a total war tactic.

Direct attacks against civilians are forbidden by the laws of war, but they are common in modern war. The British blockaded German shipping in World War I and caused great hardship and starvation among the civilian population. The Allies bombed German cities in World War II, and the Germans bombed Great Britain and many of the cities of Europe. All these are total war tactics.

Battlefield Tactics

Shortly after the end of the Persian Gulf War, Congressional investigators found that some U.S. bulldozer units had deliberately buried thousands of Iraqi troops alive even as the Iraqis tried to surrender. The investigators and other commentators criticized this method of fighting as a violation of international law; it was also a violation of orders, which directed the units to bypass Iraqi fortifications.

Burying opposing troops alive is not an accepted battlefield tactic, but it is not surprising that a modern army did it. Modern armies often use equally destructive tactics. Some, like "free-fire zones" (areas in which the U.S. forces in Vietnam were authorized to kill anything that moved), violate international law. Others, like the use of "anti-personnel" weapons (weapons which are specifically designed to wound and maim rather than to kill), may not.

The Christian "Just War" theory, which is discussed in more detail in Chapter 4, provides standards not just for deciding when war is justified, but for deciding which tactics are acceptable. If you accept this or some other form of "just war" theory, you've probably got your own ideas about which tactics are acceptable and which are not. If you reject all wars, you may wonder why you should worry about whether particular tactics are acceptable, but it's an important issue for everyone. It's best if the fighting never starts; but once it *does* start, it is likely to be less destructive if armies follow international law. In the long run, that benefits all sides.

Unconventional Wars and Weapons

In the modern world, it's very difficult to decide which wars are "conventional" and which are not. Is bombing a city "conventional"? Some think that it is because most modern armies do it; others think it is not because it may violate international law. This section discusses two types of unconventional warfare and some issues related to modern war for you to think about.

Guerrilla Warfare

Guerrilla warfare got its name from the Spanish armed resistance to Napoleon's armies. Guerrillas are soldiers who live among the civilian population, usually supported by them (willingly or not), and operate by small, fast attacks against "conventional" forces and by sabotage. A conventional army usually has trouble defeating a guerrilla force because guerrilla soldiers disappear into the population when they aren't fighting

Because it's often difficult or impossible to tell the soldiers from the civilians, war against guerrilla forces (called "counter-insurgency warfare") doesn't involve battles as we usually understand them. A counter-insurgency force attacks not only the guerrilla forces, but the population which supports them. So, for instance, crops were destroyed in Vietnam to try to cut off the guerrillas' food supplies. Jungles were "defoliated" (sprayed with a powerful weed killer) to make it harder for the guerrillas to hide. Entire villages were evacuated and destroyed. And so on. The same kinds of tactics have been used by Soviet armies in Afghanistan, the Rhodesian army before majority rule in that country, and the South African army.

This isn't surprising. Many military experts think that one guerrilla can defeat as many as ten conventional soldiers by using stealth, harassment, and civilian support. Many others think that fighting guerrillas will be part of the main work of Western armies in the future. This is the opinion not only of people in the peace movement, who oppose counter insurgency war, but even of military thinkers who support it.

Terrorism

Political analysts often say that another form of unconventional warfare is *terrorism.* Terrorists and terrorist groups try to create fear by acts of random (or seemingly random) violence. It is an old political tactic with long historical roots (the "Assassins," for example, whose name gave us the word *assassin,* were a terrorist group in the Middle Ages). In today's world, terrorists may use explosives, guns, or other modern weapons to attack buildings, political leaders, or innocent bystanders.

Terrorist attacks are not war by this book's definition, but as a CO you may be asked what you would do about terrorism. You don't have to have a solution to the problems of terrorism, political violence, and other violence in order to be a CO. Nobody really knows what to do about these problems.

You can get help in understanding the history and nature of terrorism from some of the books suggested in "A Short Course on War" and "Further Reading" in the Appendices to this book.

Unconventional Weapons

Part of the rationale for the Persian Gulf War was the fear that Iraq had developed chemical (gas) and biological (germ) weapons and was trying to develop nuclear weapons. (For a discussion of nuclear weapons, see Chapter 8.) United Nations inspectors found no proof that Iraq had developed germ weapons, but in the late 1980s the Iraqi government actually used poison gas to suppress a revolt among its own people.

Iraq, however, was neither the first nor the only country to experiment with or use gas warfare. Armies on both sides used gas in World War I. Though outlawed by a Geneva convention following that war, gas remained in the arsenals of many countries. As this book went to press, the United States maintained a large stockpile of poison gas. The U.S. military used tear gas in Vietnam. And both sides in the Cold War developed deadly gas for use in combat.

During the Cold War period the U.S. also funded extensive research on germ warfare. Because much of this research was carried on in secret, no one knows exactly how extensive it was or what stockpiles, if any, of biological weapons the U.S. maintains.

Both gas and germ warfare violate international law. Both would kill indiscriminately, and neither could be controlled once begun. Gas would eventually disperse into the air, polluting the atmosphere, and would cause a great deal of damage before it did. Disease, once launched on the population, might spread out of control and cause an epidemic. And, though both may never be used, they pose a threat to the public even if merely maintained in storage. A gas leak, for example, would cause great destruction without regard for whether it was wartime or peacetime.

War Without Killing

During the Persian Gulf War, officers in the military sometimes asked conscientious objectors whether they would object to weapons which overcame the enemy without killing anyone. They suggested that the U.S. was developing such weapons and that they might make war acceptable.

This sounds farfetched, particularly since most modern weapons are *more* likely to kill than the weapons of years ago. But it raises an important issue for you to think about: What exactly is war all about, and what makes it wrong? The Chinese military philosopher Sun Tzu argued that the highest form of the "art of war" consisted of defeating one's opponent without battle— by better tactics which brought about surrender before the fighting started. Would you find war acceptable if armies decided battles without fighting?

This book can't answer that question for you. As you

think about war, however, keep in mind that war is not necessarily about killing as such. You can view killing and wounding the soldiers in an opposing army as a means to an end. The goal of a military force is to *impose its will* on its opponents. Sun Tzu suggests that an army can do this without killing, by using the *threat* of force.

Do you think it is okay for one country or army to impose its will on another? Does it matter what tactics it uses to do so? Does war always involve the threat of force, even if no one is actually killed or wounded? Your answers to these questions will help you to answer the question of whether you should be part of war.

A Final Word

As you think about conscientious objection, keep in mind the obvious: Nobody is asking you to fight in battles like Waterloo. War today is *modern* war, with all that that implies. It's unlikely that the world will abolish all modern weapons and tactics. If the nations could agree to that, they probably could also agree to abolish war itself.

Just as nobody is asking you to fight in an 18th-Century army, so nobody is asking you to fight in a war in which nobody is killed or wounded. Such a war may be the dream of military theorists, but in the real world, military planners assume that soldiers and civilians will be killed and wounded when the shooting starts.

In the real world, modern armies have caused untold destruction. Since World War II, over 35 million people have died in "conventional" wars. Can you be part of this kind of killing and destruction? That's the real question for you to decide.

Things to Think About

☞ Do you think modern war is different from earlier wars? Does that make a difference to your beliefs about older wars?

☞ What do you think about terrorism? Do you think it is ever justified? If so, why? If not, why not?

☞ Do you see any difference between guerrilla fighters and conventional soldiers? If so, what is the difference?

☞ Do you think that chemical weapons are worse than conventional weapons like artillery? If so, why? If not, why not?

Ideas for Papers

✍ Compare two battles, one older (such as Waterloo) and one modern (for instance, from World War II). What weapons did the armies use? How did their weapons affect the fighting, the length of the battle, the numbers killed and wounded?

✍ Analyze the use of "smart" weapons. Compare how they are supposed to work with their actual performance in the Persian Gulf War.

✍ Analyze the use of gas in warfare and why it has been outlawed.

Chapter 8
You and Nuclear War

Wars have always been deadly. In the seventeenth century, eight million people died in Germany alone during the Thirty Years War (1618-1648). The American Civil War killed 529,000 on both sides; World War I, ten million; World War II, 38 million.

But worst of all for the world of today were the deaths of 100,000 caused by a single nuclear explosion at Hiroshima.

The Hiroshima bombing marked the beginning of the atomic age in warfare. Many people think that it changed the rules of war for all time. Today a major war between nuclear powers could mean the end, not just of one nation or of civilization, but of humanity itself. That has never been true before.

What Nuclear War Would Do

No one knows what a full-scale nuclear war would be like. Some experts believe that 100-170 million Americans would die in such a conflict. Survivors would have little or no food and would face great danger from radiation. Nuclear fallout might cover much of the country. And, as we are learning today, those who lived through a nuclear war might die of cancer years later or have stillborn or deformed children.

Nuclear war would not only destroy cities and people. It would poison the environment—perhaps beyond repair. Even a small amount of radiation can be dangerous. A 450-rem dose is fatal to half of those who are exposed to it. A nuclear war would release millions—perhaps billions—of rem into the air. Could the earth, air, and water absorb so much radiation and still support life? Even the experts cannot say, but many believe they could not.

The nuclear weapons in the world's arsenals have enough power to kill the entire human race *more than ten times over.* And of all countries, the U.S. has the largest number of nuclear warheads and missiles.

How Large Is the Bomb?

Figures like these don't give much idea what a nuclear attack would really be like. It's hard even to understand how big today's nuclear warheads are. But you can get an idea by thinking of tons of TNT. A moderate-sized conventional bomb has the power of 1/2 ton of TNT. The largest conventional bomb has the power of 10 tons of TNT.

The explosive power of nuclear weapons is measured in *thousands* or *millions* of tons of TNT power. For instance, a small nuclear bomb has the power of 10 kilotons, or 10,000 tons of TNT. The Hiroshima bomb had the power of 10,000-20,000 tons of TNT.

Even a small modern Inter-Continental Ballistic Missile (ICBM), however, makes the Hiroshima bomb look tiny. Polaris and Minuteman missiles carry warheads with the power of 1-2 megatons of TNT. That is 1,000,000-

2,000,000 tons of TNT power.

To give yourself an idea how large this really is, you can imagine a very long freight train. In order to hold one megaton of TNT, the train would have to be made up of 300 box cars. At full speed, the train would take six hours to pass as you watched it go by.

An H-Bomb in Manhattan

Even a one-megaton bomb is not very large for a nuclear warhead. Some land-based missiles and bombs carried in aircraft are 15-25 megatons in size, or 100 times the size of the Hiroshima bomb. Nuclear bombs this large—along with thousands of "smaller" bombs—could and would be used against cities in a nuclear war.

What would happen if a 20-megaton bomb fell in midtown Manhattan? One study describes the devastation that such a bomb would cause.

First, the sky would fill with a bluish-white fireball whose heat at the center would be nearly that of the sun itself. This fireball would expand until it was four miles wide.

> To the west it spans the Hudson River; to the east it reaches across the river to Queens. Times Square, Rockefeller Center, big ocean liners, Central Park, the United Nations are instantly incinerated.

Following the fireball would come a pressure wave traveling at speeds many times that of sound. It would spread from the center of the explosion, crushing everything in its path until it slowly lost its force. Winds, some at thousands of miles per hour, would follow the pressure wave and destroy anything that might be left standing.

This wind, rushing outward, would create a vacuum

at the center of the city. When the outward wind had lost its force, the vacuum at the center would trigger a reverse windstorm. The reverse winds would rush back to the center of the city, fanning any flames which the first explosion had started—whether from the explosion itself or from broken gas mains, short circuits, upset stoves, or other causes. The fire department could not cope with such fires, for there might be more than a million separate fires to begin with. There would be no water, and most fire fighters would be dead or badly burned. The fires would condense into a firestorm which, like a fire in a fireplace, would suck in air from around its edges, creating even more hurricane-force winds.

Six million people would die either instantly or within a few days.

Even far from "ground zero" (the center of the blast) there would be immense damage. At twenty-seven miles from ground zero, a person might receive third-degrees burns; at thirty-two miles, second-degree burns; at forty-five miles, first-degree bums. Those with second- and third-degree burns would probably also die.

These would be only the first effects of the blast. Since all medical facilities would be crippled, those who somehow survived the explosion might die slowly and painfully over the next few weeks. If they did not die then, exposure to radiation might bring on cancer. And their unborn children might be deformed or even dead at birth.

"Nuclear Strategy"

Many people, including many military officers, believe that destruction like this makes large-scale war too dangerous to risk. Rear Admiral Gene LaRocque (U.S. Navy, Ret.) put it this way:

> There is no defense. We [couldn't] defend ourselves against [an adversary's] missiles, and [our adversaries couldn't] defend themselves against our missiles. There's nowhere to hide.

Lord Mountbatten, who fought in World Wars I and 11, said:

> As a military man who has given half a century of active service I say in all sincerity that the nuclear arms race has no military purpose. Wars cannot be fought with nuclear weapons.

Not only would nuclear war be destructive, it wouldn't accomplish anything. It would be what military theorists call "absolute war"—war which can only destroy, not gain any political end.

But "nuclear strategists" don't talk much about what would happen if there were a nuclear war. They argue that nuclear weapons are useful for "deterrence"—for preventing war. The idea of "deterrence" seems simple: If you have enough weapons, you can frighten your opponents so that they won't use their weapons. So, for instance, if U.S. planners think another country has a bomb that would destroy U.S. missiles, the U.S. will try to build missiles that another country's bomb couldn't destroy. They will do this because they think that if they don't they will lose their "deterrent" and be attacked. A nation feels that it will lose its "deterrent" if the other side gets an "advantage" in the arms race.

The trouble with this idea, according to its critics, is that it doesn't work. When each side can destroy the other ten times over, does "advantage" have any meaning? For example, even if all U.S. land-based guided missiles were destroyed in a surprise attack, the U.S. could still destroy hundreds of cities and kill millions of people using missiles mounted on submarines. Who has the "advantage" here? *Both* sides would suffer immense destruction. Would there be a winner in such an exchange of missiles? Even for those who support "deterrence," it's hard to say.

"Deterrence" is a strange idea—and a new one in military history. Before there were nuclear weapons, most countries built weapons with the idea that they might be used. Now, many weapons are built with the idea that they won't be used, except to frighten the other side. But the more weapons there are, and the more countries that have them, the more dangerous the world is. Arms races and the spread of nuclear weapons increase tensions. And they don't prevent wars like Vietnam and Afghanistan.

Meanwhile, say their critics, nuclear weapons cost a great deal of money. They make the world more dangerous. New computers and other "automatic retaliation" devices have made war by accident more and more likely. In 1979, for instance, U.S. forces were alerted for nuclear war four times. All four alerts were caused by computer malfunctions. Despite the end of the Cold War, many of the same dangerous systems remain in place.

Nuclear "deterrence," the critics say, is too dangerous. The only safe alternative is peace and full nuclear disarmament.

Nuclear Pacifism

Many people have come to agree with LaRocque and Mountbatten about nuclear war. Some have become "nuclear pacifists," who believe that use of nuclear weapons can never be justified. Or they may have rejected all wars—for instance, because they believe a large conventional war would soon become a nuclear holocaust.

All three groups of people agree on one thing—nuclear war and nuclear weapons are the greatest danger we have ever faced. Most believe that nuclear war itself—not the Russians or the Americans or any other nuclear power—is the enemy.

You can't qualify as a conscientious objector just because you object to nuclear war. But it's true that nuclear weapons have changed the nature of war and made it dangerous beyond its own destructiveness. Many countries, including the U.S., Russia, Great Britain, and India, have nuclear weapons; others, such as South Africa and Israel, are believed by experts to have developed them in secret; while an unknown number of others are working to develop them. A "conventional" war between two countries with nuclear weapons could quickly become a nuclear war. In a tense world, any war, even a small one, could become a confrontation and bring a nuclear holocaust closer.

So, if you are against nuclear war, you may find that you're also against all modern wars. And modern wars are the ones that matter most.

But the Cold War Has Ended...

The end of the Cold War has led to many proposals for partial nuclear disarmament by the U.S. and the former Soviet Union. These proposals and the agreements which they may lead to are steps away from nuclear danger. But they won't make the world safe from nuclear war. As you've seen above, the U.S. and the former Soviet Union weren't the only nuclear powers during the Cold War. And nuclear technology is spreading despite efforts like the Nuclear Non-Proliferation Treaty. The more countries which have nuclear weapons, the greater the danger, even if the U.S. and the former Soviet Union destroy a great many of their weapons.

And there is another danger. Small nuclear devices can be made very easily and cheaply, and they can still cause enormous destruction. "Nuclear terrorism" isn't just a figment of a thriller writer's imagination. A nuclear bomb small enough to fit into a suitcase could still kill and sicken thousands of people and destroy hundreds of buildings.

It could also cause a major war. You probably learned in your history class that World War I started when the Austrian Archduke Franz Ferdinand was assassinated in Sarajevo in 1914. That was a terrorist action. Its consequences included over ten million deaths in the first great war of this century. If a terrorist resorted to a nuclear bomb, the results would also be unpredictable—and very dangerous.

No Going Back

In war throughout history, there has never been any going back. Gunpowder might have been "limited" at first, but by World War I the only limits on its use were caused by lack of supplies. Tanks, the airplane, the submarine, even the railroad—all changed war for all time. So have nuclear weapons.

Nuclear strategists talk a lot about "limited" nuclear war, "tactical" nuclear weapons, and other ways in which a nuclear war would not be an all-out holocaust. But keeping nuclear weapons under control, once the shooting started, would be very difficult. Lord Mountbatten thought it might be impossible:

> I have never been able to accept the ... belief that ... nuclear weapons can be categorized in terms of their tactical or strategic purposes. I know how impossible it is to pursue military operations in accordance with fixed plans and agreements. In warfare the unexpected is the rule and no one can anticipate what an opponent's reaction will be to the unexpected.

No matter what the strategists may think now, Mountbatten says, if there were a war many things could not be predicted. And, though that might mean there would be no nuclear war at all, it might mean just the opposite. Is the risk worth taking? You will need to think about this question as you decide where you stand.

You and Nuclear War

When you're thinking about yourself and nuclear war, you need to ask yourself a number of questions. Do you think that deterrence will go on working? Or is it itself a danger? Do you think a large conventional war between two nuclear powers could be kept from becoming a nuclear war? Do you think that a nuclear war could be limited?

Many people answer these questions by saying that we ought to have all the nuclear weapons we can make, and be prepared to use them. Many others say that this is wrong—that the survival of humanity is more important than "victory" (whatever that means in a nuclear war) for one nation.

What do you think?

Things to Think About

☞ Can you think of any way that a nation could win a nuclear war?

☞ Do you think the world can control the spread of nuclear weapons? How?

☞ Some people argue that every war involving nuclear-armed countries could end as a nuclear war. Do you agree?

☞ Some people argue that nuclear power is more of a threat than nuclear war. Do you agree?

Ideas for Papers

✍ Analyze the effects of the atomic bomb on Hiroshima.

✍ Write an explanation of the idea of "deterrence" and then explain why you either agree or disagree with it.

✍ Analyze how nuclear weapons manufacturing affects the environment.

Chapter 9
Force, Violence, and War

Many COs are puzzled by issues like whether it is right to use force in self-defense, whether a violent revolution can be justified, and whether there is any difference between police force and military force. Even under the law's narrow definition, you don't have to have answers to these questions to qualify as a CO. You can believe that self-defense is justified, for instance, or be against it, or not know what you would do.

But it's good to think about force and violence even though you don't have to. People who oppose your CO stand may try to trick you with questions about what you would do if you were personally attacked or about how you would resist an oppressive government. Questions about the use of force are important for everyone to think about—not just for COs.

What Is Force?

One reason why force and violence are so hard to grapple with is that "force" has many meanings. Webster's Collegiate Dictionary gives eight separate meanings to the word "force." They range from the force used by a good public speaker to the force used in war. In physics, "force" is the power which causes a body to accelerate.

Force can be applied against other nations, crowds, groups of people, or individuals. It can be violent or non-violent.

These many meanings of the word "force" make it important for you to decide for yourself which uses of force are right, and which are wrong. One thing you can't do is oppose all force. If you did, you couldn't even make a "forceful" speech, or use "forceful" arguments in discussions with your friends.

Force and Violence

Many COs begin by distinguishing between violent and non-violent force. They oppose violent force and support non-violent force. This is a useful line to draw, but you need to be clear which uses of force you think are violent and which you think are non-violent.

As you'll see below, for example, many people believe that injustice is a form of violence, even when no guns are used to enforce it. Others disagree. What's your opinion?

It isn't very useful to say simply that you're against all violence. What do you think is violent? How do you decide whether a particular use of force is violent? You don't have to have answers to these questions to be a CO, but you do need to think about them.

Even though this seems hard when it's written out on paper, you'll probably find that it's easier in practice to see where you stand. You need to think not only with your mind, but with your feelings. Often your heart will tell you what to do when your head is completely stymied.

Self-Defense

One question which nearly everyone asks a male CO is, "What would you do if your wife (or mother or granddaughter or daughter) was being raped?" For women the question would be different—the questioner might even ask what *you* would do if you were raped—but the idea would be the same. Many people think that if you can't respond nonviolently, even to a vicious assault, you can't be a CO.

This is a hard question to answer because it's really two questions: What do you think you ought to do?, and, What do you think you really would do? But these are hard questions for anyone—not just for COs. You may say you would respond non-violently, but in practice you might even kill the attacker. Someone who says he or she would probably use violence might decide in practice that non-violence is the best response.

That's true of all self-defense. You can know what you ought to do, but you can't know what you actually would do—with one major exception. If you or one of your loved ones were attacked, you probably wouldn't napalm the attacker, or dig a trench around his house and bombard him with artillery fire, or torture and kill his family. And the courts agree. For the law, as well as common sense, defending yourself in a back alley is not the same as making war.

Revolutionary Violence

In a complex, changing world, violent revolution against injustice is one of the hardest issues you will face. Revolutionary violence now ranges from the traditional overthrow of the government (like the French and

Russian revolutions) to hostage-taking or planting bombs in supermarkets. Even rioting like that in Los Angeles in 1992 may be a violent protest against injustice. What are you to make of all this? Is it right or wrong? Do you support or oppose revolutionary violence? And what kinds of violence do you mean? How—if you support some forms of violence—are they different from war?

Many people find this issue very hard because they believe that an unjust society is itself a kind of violence. Pierre Proudhon, a 19th-Century French radical, once said, "Property is theft." He was not justifying theft, but he was saying that people who have a lot often have it at the expense of others who have little or nothing. You don't have to agree with Proudhon to see that he was pointing at an issue that troubles many people—COs and non-COs alike. If you say you're against injustice, somebody is sure to ask you how you feel about revolutionary violence.

It may help if you think about the difference between supporting violence and understanding its causes. Many people, including those who believe in non-violence, get the two confused. If someone is angry, his or her natural impulse is to strike out at whatever caused the anger—or at something else that is an easy target. So, for instance, many African-Americans and Latinos in Los Angeles in 1992 lived in bad housing, had high unemployment, and felt they were victims of discrimination. When four police were acquitted of beating an African-American man during an arrest, many people in the poor neighborhoods of Los Angeles rioted. They were outraged by the court decision, of course, but there were other causes for their anger.

To understand why people are angry, however, isn't the same as saying that their violent responses are right or even sensible. Many thinkers have argued that violent means always corrupt whatever end they are seeking. And history seems to bear this out. The French Revolution led to the Reign of Terror and Napoleon; the Russian Revolution led to Stalin. Many would say that the riots in Watts (a neighborhood of Los Angeles) and other places during the 1960s led to less change than the non-violent civil rights movement—or than the Supreme Court decision outlawing racial segregation in public schools in 1954. Do you agree or disagree?

Police Force

COs are often asked if they see any difference between the police and the military. You may not, and, particularly today, that's not surprising. Often the police are used to suppress efforts for justice. Most police forces are organized very much like the military. Some police forces give their members military-style training. Specialized police units like SWAT teams use military-style tactics. And, when all else fails, the police are prepared to shoot and kill a suspect.

But, on paper at least, it's not that simple. The police are enforcing laws, many of them designed to protect the whole community from wrongdoing. They work under legal controls very different from the "laws of war." Much of their work involves enforcing traffic laws, resolving disputes between people, and other basically non-violent actions.

If a police officer shoots someone illegally, he or she may be suspended from the force or even prosecuted.

That is rarely true of soldiers in war. An army doesn't distinguish between guilty and innocent enemies. If a soldier kills a civilian—which is still technically against the laws of war—he or she may or may not face legal action. To some extent it will depend on who wins the war. Even the most famous War Crimes trials, those at Nuremberg, would have been completely different if the Axis had won the Second World War. And many actions that may be war crimes, such as "carpet bombing"—the indiscriminate dropping of bombs on an area—are now accepted military practice.

This isn't to say that you should (or shouldn't) support police force. But as you think about police force and military force, keep in mind that, even though they may be very close in practice, they are different in principle. You can be against all police force, both in practice and in principle. Or you can support the principle of police force while opposing some of the ways it is applied. You can support all police force in practice and in principle. There are good reasons for all three positions. But don't confuse police force and military force and make a tricky question even trickier.

Military Force

One real difference between police force and military force is that the police are under community control (at least on paper) and the military, when it invades another country, is not under the control of the community where it is operating. This means that, for the military, the end—the "mission," or winning the war—is most important, and the means to the end is whatever force the commanders feel is needed.

A concrete example will make this more clear. In Vietnam, villages were often "pacified"—another way of saying that the population was uprooted and taken to an internment camp, where they were questioned (often using torture) and some were killed. This was shocking to the public, but to many who knew the history of war it wasn't surprising. The military wasn't a police force. It was operating under American, not Vietnamese, orders. Its orders were to defeat an enemy. "Pacification" was one means to that end.

That's also true with other military force which you may find shocking. Sherman's March to the Sea, which cut a wide swath of burned and devastated land from Atlanta to the Georgia Coast, is today considered not only good military strategy, but an important development in the history of "total war." We are shocked by the use of poison gas, but in fact, in World War I, the only war when it was used on a large scale, gas was not a very effective weapon. (It was, however, devastating when used by Iraqi troops against Kurdish civilians in early 1990.) Artillery and machine-gun fire killed far more people than gas in World War 1. Gas is now against the "laws of war," while artillery and machine-gun fire are not. The "rights" and "wrongs" of military force aren't judged the way you would normally judge right and wrong. That's probably why you're reading this book in the first place.

Your Own Stand

No matter where you come out on the use of force, keep in mind that force—even violent force—and war are two different things. You can be puzzled about which use of force is right and which is wrong, while at the same time you may know that war is wrong. The important question in deciding whether you are a CO is where you stand on war.

Don't let tricky questions on force and violence confuse the central issue.

Things to Think About

☞ How do *you* decide whether it's right to use force?

☞ This chapter argues that war is different from other uses of force. Do you agree?

☞ How do you think oppressed people can change their situation?

☞ Do you think violence always leads to more violence?

Ideas for Papers

✎ Discuss the use of non-violent methods—such as sit-ins, boycotts, and strikes—in a movement for social change. Examples might include the civil rights movement, the labor movement, and the peace movement.

✎ Interview someone who took part in one of these movements; describe and analyze the interview.

Chapter 10
Hitler and Other Dictators

One question which you're almost sure to face—from your local board if you ever face the draft, from your neighbors, and even from yourself—is whether you would have fought against Hitler.

In a way, it's an unfair question. Many people who fought in World War II now believe that all war is wrong. Others who refused to fight now think they made a mistake and should have fought. There's nothing you can do to change what happened in Europe in 1939 or 1943—long before you were born. It's all in the past, and war today is completely different from what it was then. How can you know what you would have thought? How can anyone expect you to know?

You can try to think what you might have done if you had held your current beliefs, but even that isn't easy. People at the time had very different reactions to Hitler. They didn't know, in 1938 or 1939, what would happen in 1941 or 1945. We now see Hitler in the light of what happened later—which people at the time couldn't have done. So, though you can try to think how your beliefs would have applied then, you can't really be sure.

The courts disagree on whether you have to be sure.

If you aren't, though, there's a good chance that you can still qualify as a CO. For details, see Chapter 4.

Hitler presents a hard problem because, except for a few modern Nazis, everyone now agrees that he was responsible for great evil. And most people think of World War II as the "good" war. It's even become a fad, as you can see in any bookstore or any store that sells strategy games.

Was it really that simple? What can we learn from the history of Europe in the 1930s and 1940s? This chapter can't answer these questions for you, but it can give you a start.

Hitler as Symbol and Reality

Many people today think of Adolf Hitler as the most evil man who ever lived. Before the recent collapse of the Soviet Union, whenever the Defense Department planned a mobilization for war in Europe, it was planning how to stop a Hitler-style *Blitzkrieg* (lightning war). Visitors to St. Petersburg (formerly Leningrad) are always taken to see the monument to those who died in the Siege of Leningrad—caused, the guides remind visitors, by Hitler's armies. People in Israel today still recall Hitler's death camps. Even the name of Hitler— or his ministers like Goebbels, Himmler, and Goering— has come to mean pure evil.

This is an exaggeration, but not by much. Hitler was a ruthless man with dangerous ideas. He was the driving force behind a war which killed over 50 million people. Millions of people died in German concentration camps—six million Jews, 200,000 Gypsies, millions of gay men and lesbians, and at least a million political prisoners. Hitler is not only a symbol of evil, but, in many ways, was the reality of it as well.

Hitler and World War II

World War II is often called "Hitler's War." Some historians believe that Hitler planned to conquer most of Europe, defeat the Soviet Union, and set up a German Empire—without war if he could do it, but by making war if he could not. This is also what the public thinks: the sole cause of the war, and the reason it was fought, was Hitler.

But, like many things in history, the answer may not have been that easy. One school of historians thinks that, though Hitler meant greatly to expand German power, he didn't plan the war that actually happened. Allied policy, they say, has to share the blame for World War II.

The truth is probably somewhere between these two positions. But even if Hitler planned the war and started it by himself, a bigger question remains: Why did he come to power in the first place? And why did the German people follow his leadership? If any question is important for today, it's this.

The Coming of the War

Historians often say that World War I and World War II were really two parts of a single process. They believe the "German problem" began in the 19th Century and was still there even after the slaughter in the trenches of World War I. It led to Hitler and to World War II. In its simplest form, the "problem" was this: Germany was becoming the most powerful country in Europe, and the other countries didn't want that to happen.

World War I was the largest European war up to its time. Ten million soldiers were killed. Great Britain and France actually lost more people in World War I than in World War II. The Treaty of Versailles, in 1919, tried to prevent another such war by disarming Germany, forcing it to pay war reparations, and setting up a new system, the League of Nations, to keep the peace in Europe. At the same time, the Allies did not disarm, and the Treaty took territory from Germany. In Germany, and later on in much of Europe, most people thought the Treaty of Versailles was unfair.

During the 1920s, Germany had a domestic constitution much like that of the United States. She also had serious domestic problems. Her army had been disbanded, but thousands of ex-soldiers formed themselves into *Freikorps* (free corps), or private armies who began as border guards but later became, in many cases, right-wing political parties backed by force. War reparations were so punitive that the famous English economist John Maynard Keynes, in his book, *The Economic Consequences of the Peace,* predicted "disastrous consequences," including the possibility of another war, if the Allies actually carried out reparations policies. German inflation in the 1920s became so bad that

> Men and women rushed to spend their wages, if possible within minutes of receiving them. Notes were trundled to the stores in wheelbarrows—or baby carriages.... [T]here was resort to virtually every printing press that was capable of printing money. Notes were in literal fact churned out. And, on occasion, trade stopped as the presses fell behind in producing new bills.

During these desperate days, the United States refused

to provide financial aid to the German government (the Weimar Republic). Some years later, British, French, and American financiers like Henry Ford did advance aid to Hitler to support him as a bulwark against Communism.

The inflation ended in 1925, but in 1929 the Great Depression began. Not only America, but the rest of the Western world, suffered high unemployment and economic collapse. In Germany,

> by 1930 what had been a bothersome problem turned into an acute disaster. In just one month, January, the number of unemployed soared from 1.5 million to almost 2.5 million. From then on, the figures kept climbing steadily.

Germans blamed the unemployment on many things. Some thought war reparations caused it. Some blamed it on dishonest, incompetent politicians. Many believed Nazi propaganda that blamed it on the Jews.

Looking back, it's hard to imagine, but Hitler was a popular figure in Germany in the early 1930s. His party never received a majority in a free election, but by 1930 it had won 107 seats in the German parliament. He came to power when the President of Germany, Hindenburg, appointed him Chancellor. He reduced unemployment by increasing public spending. He built public works like the *Autobahn* (a highway system) that are remembered today. Most of all, to Germans who thought of themselves as surrounded by hostile nations, he appeared to be a welcome savior and protector. He was not. Once in power he gradually consolidated his dictatorship and escalated his campaign against the Jews, other "non-Aryan" peoples, gays, and political opponents.

Overseas, he had many sympathizers—ranging from industrialists like Henry Ford to the writer Anne Morrow Lindbergh, wife of Charles Lindbergh. In an article in *Reader's Digest*, she wrote:

> Much that is happening in Hitler's Germany is bad....
> but perhaps it will lead to some ultimate good. We, as
> Americans, do not have the moral right to judge what is
> happening.... What was pushing behind Communism?
> What's behind fascism in Italy? What's behind Naziism?
> ... Something one feels is pushing up through the crust of
> custom.... One does not know what ... some new conception of humanity and its place on earth. I believe that it is,
> in its essence, good.

Lindbergh, who devoted her life to humanitarian causes, later came to regret these words. But she wasn't alone. Many people deceived themselves about Hitler. Many others secretly agreed with him.

Appeasement

Today we have been taught to think of "appeasement" as a kind of cowardice. Most people believe that the "appeasers" gave in to Hitler's demands, especially at Munich in 1938, and helped to bring on the war. Negotiations between countries today have become much more difficult because neither side wants to be accused of "appeasement. "

The truth isn't quite so simple. Hitler made many demands in the late 1930s, but the Munich agreement, which gave him parts of Czechoslovakia, was actually a British and French proposal. And it had much public support. "[F]ew causes have been more popular. Every newspaper [in Britain] applauded the Munich settlement with the exception of Reynolds' News." In the 19th and early 20th centuries, many great powers settled their differences by dividing up smaller powers or colonies. You may think this was very wrong, but it was common. British Prime Minister Neville Chamberlain wasn't an advocate of nonviolence, and the partition of Czechoslovakia wasn't an example of nonviolence or the "failure" of peacemaking. It was, in many ways, a continuation of traditional diplomacy—but even more cynical than most such agreements.

A Dilemma

It's easy to look back and criticize Chamberlain, who proposed the Munich settlement. But at the time, Chamberlain was faced with a terrible dilemma. He couldn't have known what would happen in the future. He couldn't have known whether a "firm stand" would have stopped Hitler. We don't even know that today, though many people assume that it would have. What Chamberlain did know was that his country had been through the most bloody war in history in 1914-1918. The Munich settlement was his way of avoiding another disastrous war. It didn't, of course, work out that way.

When a leader like Hitler is in power, armed with a mass army, there isn't any good solution to the problems he creates. World War II killed over 50 million people and laid waste much of Europe and Asia. It's hard to think of this as good, even though many people do. So it wasn't a choice of a "good" war or a "bad" non-war. *Both* choices were bad because each might have led to great suffering.

It's possible that a different stand by the Allies at

Munich would have prevented or postponed World War II. It's also possible that the war would have started sooner if the Allies had threatened Hitler with military force. No one will ever know. What we do know today is that Hitler might never have come to power if the Allies had followed different policies after World War I—for instance, if they'd followed through on their pledges about disarmament and the League of Nations and had helped the struggling Weimar Republic in the 1920s. And we can see how the policies that they did follow laid the groundwork for the crisis of 1938 and the war that followed.

Hitler didn't just happen. Allied policy, including that of the United States, must share a lot of the blame for Hitler's rise to power and the damage that he did.

Even when their policies had failed, the Allies didn't at first see the war as a crusade. Going to war didn't, for instance, stop the Holocaust; and before the war, the Allies had done little or nothing to save the Jews of Europe. Britain declared war when Germany invaded Poland, but "as late as 1940, when France fell, some British political leaders gave thought and utterance to coming to terms with Hitler and letting him be." The United States kept out of the war until the Japanese attack on Pearl Harbor in 1941. Even then, Hitler declared war on the U.S. before the U.S. declared war on Germany.

The Horrors of War

Like most modern wars, World War II was a total war, as described in Chapter 7. It aimed not only at the enemy's armies, but at the people of the enemy's country. So it's not surprising that millions of civilians were killed.

Hitler's armies and his later policies were certainly more cruel than those of the Allies. Hitler ordered the Holocaust. Toward the end of the war, he gave orders for all of Germany to be leveled rather than surrender. And he destroyed himself by his own suicide, and millions of soldiers and civilians by suicidal strategies like his attack on the Soviet Union. At the same time, German soldiers, following policies laid down by Hitler and Himmler, became known for their abusive treatment of prisoners and civilians.

Yet many of the policies of the Allies caused terrible damage—more, according to many historians, than was needed to win the war. The so-called "area bombing" campaign—which today would be called "saturation bombing" or "carpet bombing"—is an example. In 1940, the British set out to destroy German military targets—oil refineries, munitions plants, etc.—by bombing raids. They soon found that, if they flew by day, their bombers would be shot down. And if they flew by night, their bombers didn't have the equipment to bomb accurately. Rather than give up the bombing raids, Bomber Command changed its targets to German cities. This was supposed to break German morale and win the war.

In fact, "area bombing" probably did no such thing, any more than German bombing of British cities broke English morale.

> Did the bombers win the war? ... The answer ... is no. The German armies were fatally defeated by the Russians in July 1943 and at that point the bomber onslaught had

barely begun and had caused no decisive damage.

What the bombing did do was kill hundreds of thousands of civilians and destroy hundreds of German cities—many, like Dresden, of cultural but not military importance. The bombing campaign was controversial even during the war. Its critics ranged from pacifists to military thinkers like Liddell Hart. This doesn't, of course, prove that the Nazis were really "good" and the Allies really "bad"—or even that, morally, there was nothing to choose between them. But it shows that, in modern war, nobody's hands are clean. Often *both* sides choose tactics which are morally questionable and may even—as carpet bombing of cities does—violate international law. That is the nature of modern war.

The Holocaust

Many people believe that the war against Germany stopped Hitler's campaign to exterminate the Jews of Europe. And that's true enough. After Germany had been defeated and Hitler had killed himself, the Allied troops liberated the extermination camps. Many of the soldiers wept uncontrollably at what they saw.

What these soldiers did not know was that, before the war and during it, many of the Allied countries had done little or nothing to help save the Jews or other threatened peoples like the Gypsies. Before the war,

> No country could be found willing to take substantial numbers of Jews; the British barred Palestine to them except in small numbers ...; the Americans ... require[d] certificates of birth which few German Jews possessed and none could ask for from a German official ...; a Bill to permit 20,000 Jewish children to enter the United States was killed by a "patriotic" lobby in the Congress on

the grounds that it offended against the sanctity of family ties.

Before the war, no country did very much to help. And the war didn't stop the Holocaust until six million Jews and millions of other peoples—gays, lesbians, Gypsies, Hitler's political opponents, and many others—had died in Nazi death camps.

In fact, after the war began, Hitler's campaign against "inferior" races actually grew more intense, even diverting resources from the war effort. The first concentration camp, at Dachau, had been set up in 1933 to hold not only Jews but Hitler's political opponents. The death camp at Auschwitz was set up in 1939, but it was not until well after the start of the war that the Nazis decided to go ahead with the "final solution." Historians have found no written order for the Holocaust, but it is likely that the decision was reached in January, 1941.

On August 8, 1942, Gerhart Riegner of the World Jewish Congress reported on Hitler's extermination plans to the United States government. At first American officials didn't believe the report. And even after it was confirmed, they didn't try to organize a rescue effort. One critic says,

> As [Hitler] moved ... toward the total destruction of the Jews, the government and the people of the United States remained bystanders. Oblivious to the evidence which poured from official and unofficial sources, Americans went about their business unmoved and unconcerned.

As the war went on, the death camps worked faster and faster.

What can we learn from the Holocaust? Although the war finally ended the Holocaust, starting the war did not prevent it. It may, in fact, have intensified the killing. Nor did the war start the Holocaust. If there had been no war, the Nazis might have killed or driven out millions of victims anyway. And Hitler's attempt at killing an entire people (now called genocide)—though it was the most terrible—was not the first. In the middle ages, Jews were often slaughtered, driven from their homes, and confined in ghettos. Between 1915 and 1918, the Turkish government massacred two million Armenians. And there have been other examples throughout history—including the Americas, where millions of Native Americans have died as a result of extermination campaigns.

One lesson of the Holocaust is that racial, religious, and ethnic hatred are always dangerous—and that evil things happen in the world. The question for you is whether your best response to evil is to participate in war. During the Holocaust, thousands of Europeans hid Jews in their homes or helped them escape destruction. From them you can learn that you don't have to fight in order to be brave and work against evil.

Another Hitler Today?

When you're thinking about Hitler, you'll probably ask yourself whether another Hitler is possible today. After all, even if you wanted to fight the historical Hitler, you couldn't. He's been dead for many years, and from 1946 to 1990 the "German problem" seemed of little importance because of the Cold War.

Part of the Cold War was the threat of nuclear war. Even after the end of the Cold War, the major powers are keeping enormous numbers of nuclear weapons.

And that makes today completely different from 1939.

Hitler wasn't completely sane. He had no regard for human life. If he had had nuclear weapons, he would probably have used them. In 1939, he could threaten the whole of Europe without nuclear weapons. Today, a Hitler without nuclear weapons could still do great harm in his own country but would pose little military threat to the world. A Hitler with the U.S. or Soviet arsenal would be a threat such as the world has never known before.

How would you—or anyone, for that matter—stop him? Other countries would probably threaten him with nuclear weapons. If war came, it would be nuclear, and it wouldn't matter very much whether you or anyone else decided to fight. Hundreds of millions would be dead before the armies could march. This would "stop" a new Hitler. It would also "stop" much— probably most—of the human race.

Many people think that a new Hitler is less of a danger to the world than "sane" world leaders with their fingers on the nuclear button. What do you think?

Saddam Hussein and Hitler

After Iraqi troops invaded Kuwait in August, 1990, President Bush called Iraqi President Saddam Hussein "the new Hitler." This made for rousing speeches, but most historians said it was not accurate—that Saddam was in no way the threat to the world that Hitler had been. The Iraqi army was much smaller than the 1939 German army, for one thing, and its weapons were no match for the sophistication and power of the Allied arsenal. And, though Saddam was a terrible dictator who attacked and killed his own people, the destruction he caused was not nearly as great as that of Hitler, or of Stalin, who killed an estimated 35 million people during his rule in the Soviet Union.

There's another major difference between Saddam Hussein and Hitler. Until August, 1990, the West *supported* Saddam, even to the point of supplying him with weapons to help in the ten-year Iran-Iraq War (1979-1989). No one talked about Hitler or the "lessons of history" when discussing Iran and Iraq. Saddam became "the next Hitler" when the President needed to build support for the Gulf War.

Learning from History

The lessons of history aren't always what the speechwriters say they are. As you decide what you're going to do, you need to be skeptical whenever a politician says that history teaches us this lesson or that lesson. Be skeptical even of the "lessons of history" in this chapter. Look it up for yourself in the books listed under "Further Reading." Ask yourself whether the people who cite the "lessons of history" are telling the truth or merely trying to influence the public.

There's no doubt that many of the world's governments have been headed by dangerous leaders. And many have been totalitarian. Being a conscientious objector doesn't mean that you have to ignore the evils of dictatorship or the dangers of expansionist military policies. In fact, you may find that you're more consistent on these issues than the government. Remember that Saddam Hussein was our "friend" until 1990, when he became "the next Hitler."

We can learn a lot from history. But, in a world of nuclear weapons, shortages, and interdependent nations, history can't tell us much about the future. And it can't tell you what your conscience requires. It's the future and your conscience you need to be concerned about.

Things to Think About

☞ Do you think Hitler's rise to power could have been prevented? How?

☞ Do you think another Hitler is possible today or in the future?

☞ What lessons do *you* draw from the history of Hitler and World War II?

Ideas for Papers

✍ Describe one of the non-violent efforts to save Jews from the Holocaust—for example in Le Chambon (see "Further Reading," in this book) or Denmark.

✍ Interview a person who fought in World War II and analyze the conversation.

✍ Interview a person who was a conscientious objector during World War II and analyze the conversation.

Chapter 11
If the Country Were Attacked

The question of Hitler is probably the hardest one when you're thinking about conscientious objection. Almost as difficult is the question, "Would you fight if the country were attacked?"

It's a hard question for three reasons. You can't know what your beliefs will be in the future. When your next-door neighbor or your friends ask the question, they usually don't say what kind of attack they mean. And hidden in this question is another: Don't you love your country enough to help it when it's threatened?

To be a conscientious objector, you don't have to know what you would do in the future. But you may want to think about your position. There's no way to do this that will work for everyone. Some people try to think of wars that might happen and ask themselves what they would do. This chapter tries to see what is really likely. For the law on hypothetical questions, read Chapter 4.

Real and Imaginary Attacks

The last time the United States was attacked was 1941, when the Japanese bombed Pearl Harbor. Although some historians now believe that U.S. officials could have prevented the attack, Congress and the public didn't know this at the time. Most supported a declaration of war against Japan.

In the nuclear age, however, an attack like Pearl Harbor is pretty unlikely. An enemy powerful enough to attack the U.S. would probably use nuclear bombs and missiles, and the war that resulted could be over in half an hour. So another Pearl Harbor—an attack on the U.S. which led to a long conventional war—is very unlikely.

You could even say it is impossible in the nuclear age. If the U.S. were attacked with nuclear missiles, it would respond with nuclear missiles. If it were invaded by a conventional army, it would still probably launch nuclear missiles against the invader's home territory. In either case the war would probably be over very quickly, though a great many people would be killed and injured, and the environment would be badly, possibly irreparably, damaged.

But even supposing that neither side used nuclear weapons, how likely is a direct attack on U.S. territory?

An attack over land seems pretty unlikely. Our only land neighbors are Canada and Mexico. The U.S. has had unarmed borders with both for over a hundred years.

Before 1991, your friends might have asked, What about the Russians? The Soviet Union has now disbanded, but even when it was at the height of its power, a Soviet invasion of the U.S. would have been a military disaster. The Soviets never had the planes and ships to mount such an attack. Troops might have come across the Bering Straits in Alaska, but attacking the continental U.S. from a base in Alaska would have meant marching thousands of miles through Canada. Cuba, which might have provided a base for an attack, is 90 miles from the Florida coast. And getting a large military force to Cuba from the Soviet Union wouldn't have been easy.

With or without a base in Cuba, a "conventional" Soviet invasion of the U.S. would have faced problems greater than any military operation in history. If the invasion force traveled by ship, the weather, the chance that the beaches would be defended, and the long distance to be covered would probably have stopped it before it started. If the attackers traveled by air, the cost in fuel would have been enormous. Thousands of airplanes would have been needed to carry hundreds of thousands of soldiers, their supplies, thousands of tanks and guns, and millions of tons of ammunition. And what would the soldiers have eaten when they arrived? How would they have kept from running out of ammunition? To solve these problems, hundreds or even thousands of planes would have needed to fly the Atlantic *every day.*

All this would be true even if the United States resisted the invasion nonviolently—for instance, by hiding or destroying food supplies. A military operation, no matter how it's resisted, needs a good supply line. Hundreds of military campaigns have broken down because the soldiers had no ammunition and no food. The most famous is probably Napoleon's invasion of Russia in 1812. Napoleon's armies left for Russia with more than 400,000 men; they returned with fewer than 200,000. Most died of cold and starvation.

Military historians now consider Napoleon's march to Moscow one of the most foolish plans in history. Yet the problems facing Napoleon were simple compared with those that would face an army attacking the U.S. over water. No general would plan such an operation. If one proposed it seriously, he would probably be removed from his post and sent on a long vacation.

Provoked and Unprovoked

When they ask you about an attack on the country, your friends are probably thinking of an unprovoked attack. But politics and military affairs are more complex than that. Suppose that, in 1970, the North Vietnamese government had bombed San Francisco and mined San Francisco Bay. Would this have been an unprovoked attack? You'd probably say it wasn't because the U.S. had been bombing Hanoi and mining North Vietnamese harbors since the late 1960s. Would you fight if there were such an attack?

It's hard to imagine a future attack on this country that would not result in some way from its policies. We like to think of the U.S. as a peaceful country, but in fact, since World War II, this country has used or threatened military force over 200 times. In some cases, like Korea and Vietnam, U.S. troops have fought long wars. The U.S. has invaded countries like Grenada, Panama, and Iraq, and they have bombed countries like Libya and Iraq. Sometimes the U.S. has sent an aircraft carrier or moved a battalion of Marines. And in the Cuban missile crisis of 1962, the U.S. actually threatened a nuclear attack on the Soviet Union.

What Could You Do?

Critics of COs often like to talk about scenes of rape, pillage, and destruction and ask COs what they would do. But war always involves destruction. A nuclear war, which would be the most destructive of all, would also be a war in which your willingness to fight would matter least. It would be over quickly, and the military probably wouldn't even have time to mobilize.

Unlikely as it is, a conventional attack on the U.S. would bring the horrors of war to this country's territory for the first time since the Civil War. The military would have time to mobilize. And you might change your mind about fighting, as people have done in the past. But if you still felt you couldn't fight, you could do much to relieve the suffering which the war would cause. You could tend the wounded, try to find shelter for people whose homes had been destroyed, and many other actions—all without being part of the military. And you could, if you wished, help organize non-violent resistance to the invaders.

"Vital Interests"

Another kind of "attack" on the U.S.—and a much more likely one—is an attack on the country's "vital interests." In 19th-Century Europe, "vital interests" meant colonial interests. Or a country might feel its "interests" were being attacked when another country tried to change the balance of power. More and more lately, however, the "vital interests" of the U.S. have come to mean natural resources like oil that are supplied by other countries.

But is war for oil likely to succeed? The Persian Gulf War (1991) was supposed, among other things, to protect Western oil supplies from an expansionist Iraq. But even at the height of its power, Iraq controlled only

7% of the world's oil reserves. Even more important, selling oil was Iraq's only source of revenue. It needed to sell oil. It couldn't have withheld its oil from the market for very long because it couldn't afford to do so. So there never was a long-term threat of oil "blackmail."

Is a threat to the oil supply really an attack on the U.S.? And would war be a sensible response to it? What about alternatives—like using less oil? During the buildup to the Gulf War, many people said the U.S. ought to be using less oil, yet as late as 1992 we still had no national energy conservation program.

Three Positions on War

Most people take one of three stands on war. The first position is that every U.S. war is a defensive war. Probably some of your friends—and your local draft board, if you ever face the draft—believe this. Even the government wants people to believe it. The Pentagon, after all, is called the Department of Defense.

Chances are, if you're reading this book, that you disagree.

The second position, which most people take, is that some wars are defensive and justified, and others are not. But what, in the modern world, is a defensive war? Before you conclude that any war is defensive, you have to know how it started and what U.S. policies led up to it. Often the public doesn't learn the full story until years later. This makes it very hard to judge which wars are defensive and which are not.

And how likely is an unprovoked attack on the country? As you've seen, it's not likely at all. But if an unprovoked attack is very unlikely, then, in practice, people who would fight only a defensive war are pretty close to people who take the third position: rejection of all wars. In fact, the two groups are the same on one point: neither group really knows what its views would be in a future war.

In the 1930s, hundreds of thousands of men in England signed pledges never to fight again. When war came in 1939, some of these men refused to fight, but most joined the military. Were they insincere when they pledged never to fight? Probably not. But their views changed. And they couldn't have known this would happen.

Though you know how you feel now, you can't really predict how you will feel ten years from now. That's true whether you now reject all wars or think you should support all U.S. wars. Before the Vietnam War, many Americans supported all U.S. wars. Most still do, but large numbers of people changed their minds because of the Indochina War.

How can you know what you would think in a future war? You can't. But to be a CO, you don't have to. You need to think about how you feel now—not in an imaginary future.

Are You Patriotic?

Your friends may not even have thought about what kind of attack they mean when they ask if you would defend the country. In their minds, whether or not you would fight in the military is the test of whether or not you support your country.

But it's not that simple. Very few COs are unpatriotic. Those who follow the law often feel they owe service to their country. Those who break the law often are protesting against a law they feel is undemocratic. And everyone who protests against war is protesting against U.S. policy—usually to change it for the better. If the only test of patriotism is willingness to serve in the military, then you're unpatriotic if you refuse. But that's not the only test. Or even a very good test.

In the nuclear age, as Chapter 8 pointed out, more and more weapons don't make the country more and more safe. If anything, they make it less safe because they would make war, if it comes, even more destructive.

Who, then, is patriotic? The person who believes in arms or the person who says No to the war system? Both may be and probably are. You must make your own decision based on your values—not on someone else's opinion of your patriotism.

In the modern world, too, patriotism may actually be dangerous if it leads people to think that it's all right to make war on other nations. So maybe you shouldn't be asking yourself whether you are patriotic, but whether patriotism is really a good thing.

Are You Afraid?

Many people think that COs aren't against war at all—that they're just afraid of dying. That's often what your neighbor means by asking if you would defend the country against an attack. It's a hard question because you don't always know why you do what you do.

But the fact is that *everyone* is afraid of death and of being wounded. That's why soldiers are drilled and grouped into platoons and brigades—so that, by following orders and being part of the group, they can fight in spite of their fear. It's not natural to move toward a machine gun that is firing at you, but soldiers are sometimes ordered to do it. Many of them would run away if their actions weren't almost automatic. Or if they were alone and didn't feel pressure from the others in their unit.

Most soldiers today, in any case, don't see combat at all. They're support troops—clerks, mechanics, etc. And when there's no war going on, the greatest chance of death in the military is from an accident.

If you're disturbed by the question of cowardice, don't let it worry you. You're not alone. The real question for you is not how you feel about dying, but how you feel about killing.

Things to Think About

☞ Do you agree that an attack on the United States is unlikely? Why or why not?

☞ Do you think it's important to be patriotic? Why or why not?

Ideas for Papers

✍ Some strategists think the U.S. could be defended non-violently. Read some of their books (see "Further Reading," in this book) and evaluate their arguments.

Part IV

Choosing Peace

Chapter 12
Choosing Peace in a Warlike World

If you had been a man reading the 1968 edition of this book, you wouldn't have had to ask yourself whether you needed to take a stand on war. The U.S. was at war in Vietnam, and draft calls were in the hundreds of thousands per year. The draft might have forced you to take a stand, even if you didn't particularly want to. Women, who didn't face the draft, were forced to think by the fact that there was a war going on. People by the thousands took public stands against the war. One national demonstration in 1971 drew over 400,000 people to Washington D.C.

Today the draft is on standby status. Military recruiters may visit your school, but you don't have to listen to them. Most of the time, the U.S. is not at war. Why should you take a stand against war? And how can you do it?

This chapter discusses why it is important for you to do what you can to bring about a more peaceful world. It talks about actions that some other people have taken to show the world that they opposed war. No chapter of a book, and no book, can or should tell you how to live. But if you're concerned about war, you'll probably find that your beliefs affect your life in ways you hadn't expected. If this chapter helps you to think, it will have done its job.

The End of War?

During 1990 and 1991, the Cold War ended and the Soviet Union was transformed into a commonwealth of independent republics. The U.S. cut back the size of its active forces. Many people hoped that the world would soon have peace.

The end of the Cold War seemed at first to make war less likely. But did it mean the end of war? Probably not. Less than a year before the breakup of the Soviet Union, the U.S. mobilized half a million troops for the Persian Gulf War. This wasn't a very promising beginning to an era of peace.

Over the years, people and nations have often hoped to bring about the end of war by overcoming one nation or leader which was supposed to be (or was) particularly evil and aggressive. In the early 19th Century, that leader was Napoleon. His downfall led to peace in Europe—for a time. In 1914, the villains were Germany and Kaiser Wilhelm III. The defeat of Germany in 1918 brought an uneasy peace that eventually led to the rise of Adolph Hitler and World War II. The defeat of Hitler, too, did not bring universal peace. It was followed by the Cold War and the threat of nuclear destruction.

Containing or defeating one particular leader, country, or even ideology will not end war. Nations fought each other before there was such a thing as Communism, and there were wars before the rise of capitalism. Napoleon was not the first aggressive dictator, and he was not the last. If achieving peace were as simple as winning just one more war, we would have had peace long ago.

This doesn't mean that the world will never have peace. But peace will not come automatically. It will come only as more and more people and nations move away from using war as a way of settling disputes. By thinking about whether you should be part of war, you can help that process. It may seem a small decision, but it's not. It's important for you—and for the world.

Stopping War Before It Starts

If you study the history of the Vietnam War, you'll find that the peace movement had a very strong role in stopping the war. There's no telling how long the war would have continued without public pressure to end it. And the peace movement played a major role in telling the public what was happening in Vietnam and why it should be stopped.

Despite the peace movement's best efforts, however, the war lasted for more than ten years. It killed millions of Vietnamese, both soldiers and civilians—no one knows exactly how many—and it led to 50,000 American combat deaths. The end of the war was a victory for the peace movement, but a very costly one.

One lesson of the Vietnam War—and of other wars— is that stopping a war after it has begun is very difficult and takes a lot of time. After the shooting has started, it's usually too late to prevent at least some bloodshed and killing. So it's important, even in peacetime, for people to think about war and work for peace.

Thinking About War and Peace

You can't change the world by yourself. But there are steps you can take to help yourself understand the issues and work to bring about peace. Here are some suggestions:

✔ *Keep informed.* No matter what your final stand on war, you can't make good decisions unless you understand the issues. This means some extra work, but it's well worth your time. You can get useful information and analysis from major newspapers, from the books and magazines listed at the end of this book, from computer bulletin boards like PeaceNet, and from many other sources. You can make a good start by reading some of the books listed under "A Short Course on War and Peace," in the Appendix to this book.

✔ *Decide where you stand.* Use this book and other books to help yourself think about war. Talk with people who know about these issues. Rent one or two of the films recommended in the film list at the end of this book. You probably won't reach a final position on every issue, but that's not important. Few COs, even those who have thought about these questions all their lives, ever answer every question about war. Neither do career military officers or the President of the United States.

✔ *Contact one or more of the groups listed in the Appendix.* You don't have to think about these issues alone. Most major groups in the peace movement can suggest literature for you to read; some have local branches where you can meet other concerned people and talk with them. All of them are eager to get in touch with young people who want to learn about war and peace.

✔ *Form your own group.* You don't have to be an expert

on peace to get together with other concerned people and study or work on issues that affect you, like recruiters in your school. CCCO and the other groups listed at the end of this book can help you get started.

✔ *Consider learning counseling yourself.* CCCO and some of the other groups listed in this book offer training in counseling people in the military who need discharges and people facing choices about the military. Providing this kind of help is one concrete action you can take now, regardless of whether the U.S. is at war. And even if you find that counseling isn't for you, you can learn a lot by taking the training.

Conscientious Objection in Your Life

Many people wonder just what it is that makes COs different from everybody else. There's really only one answer to this question: COs can't take part in war (or one particular war) because they believe to do so would be wrong. But just as there is no CO haircut or style of dress, there is no one set of values that is shared by all COs.

This doesn't mean that your beliefs won't affect your life. For most COs, objecting to war is part of a process of growth. It's based on a positive set of values, not just on a negative refusal to take part. Those values differ from one CO to another. And what they mean in each CO's life is different, too.

As you think about war and whether you should oppose it, you'll probably also find that you're thinking about issues like what kind of career you might pursue, what kind of food you should eat, how you use resources, and many other questions. There's no one "CO position" on these questions. For example, some COs are vegetarians; others are not. Whether if you object to war you also shouldn't eat meat is for you and you alone to decide. It's the same with other issues.

Nor is there a single "CO way of life" or lifestyle. You can express your beliefs in many ways: by working in the peace movement, by helping at a local youth center, by your choice of career, or by many other choices you make. You can even show your beliefs by how you treat your friends and neighbors. But you don't *have* to do anything unless you feel moved to do it. Becoming a conscientious objector is first of all a change in your heart and mind. What you do after you've gone through that change—and whether you go through it—is up to you. That is, after all, one thing that becoming a conscientious objector is about: making your own decisions, and following your conscience where it leads you.

Positive Choices

Many COs express their beliefs by helping others or by working for peace, the environment, or social justice. There are many ways you can do this. Here are some ideas on how you might choose to become involved.

Peace in Your School

Many schools have service programs or student groups which give time and effort to help others. For example, your school might have a chapter of Amnesty International, a group that works to free political prisoners and victims of torture. If it doesn't have one, you might consider starting one. It's the same with other programs, like after-school tutoring. Check to see whether your school already has a program—and if not, and you think such a program would be a good idea, talk with your advisor about starting one. Some students have also started peace action or discussion groups at their schools.

If military recruiters come to your school to give presentations, you may be able to arrange for a peace-oriented speaker to balance the recruiter's talk. Under the law, if your school allows recruiters to speak at your school, it must allow time for opposing viewpoints. For more information, contact CCCO or another of the groups listed at the back of this book.

Volunteering Your Time and Skills

Most community groups, churches, and non-profit agencies need and welcome volunteer help. You can live your beliefs by simply giving time (for example, stuffing mailings) or, if you have special skills, giving your expertise. For example, if you have carpentry skills, you might see whether your community has a non-profit housing group that could use your help.

By volunteering your time and skills, you learn more about the groups you work with and what they do. Your volunteer work might even lead to a job with the organization or a career in a field you didn't expect.

If you're a member of a church, one easy way to get started is to volunteer for the church. For example, if your church runs a soup kitchen for the homeless, you could sign up to staff the kitchen once or twice a month.

Serving on Boards

Non-profit and community groups are usually governed by a "Board of Directors" which makes policy for the group and makes decisions about budgets and program directions. Many of these boards are looking for younger members. Serving on a non-profit board can be a satisfying way to help a group you support while you pursue your own career.

Don't join a board unless you will have time to devote to your board service. Board members often spend a lot of their spare time serving on committees or working closely with staff to improve the organization. But if you have the time, and if you're invited, give the offer serious consideration.

Helping Careers

If you're thinking about becoming a teacher, a doctor, a nurse, a social worker, or joining some other helping profession, you will have the chance to put your beliefs into action every day. Many COs in the past have chosen professions like these because of the opportunities they give for service. Other professions, such as law, also offer opportunities to help—for instance, if you're an attorney, by representing COs who are trying to get discharged from the military.

Careers with Social Change and Non-Profit Groups

Although most of the groups that work for peace and social justice are small and have small staffs, some COs have devoted their entire careers to social change or to working for charitable agencies. If you support a particular group and want to work with it, you could start by volunteering. This won't guarantee you a paying job with the group, but volunteers with talent often get serious consideration for jobs that open up.

Most non-profit groups need staff with a variety of skills and willingness to learn and to change with the times. Nearly all need staff (and volunteers) who can operate computers. Many non-profit jobs need skills like desktop publishing, typing, bookkeeping, graphic arts, and writing. No matter where you work, these can be useful skills to have.

Living Your Convictions

As you can see, there are a lot of ways for you to live by your beliefs. Those mentioned in this section are only ideas. You don't have to work in any particular job or serve on a board to be a CO. But these suggestions will help get you started as you think about how to put your beliefs into action.

Resisting War

For some COs, following the lead of conscience means taking direct action against war. If you're a man subject to draft registration, for example, you could decide to refuse to register. That choice and what it could mean is discussed in Chapter 16 of this book.

You don't have to take direct action to be a CO, and direct action for peace usually doesn't involve breaking the law. But for some COs it may. Here are two of the many ways that COs have resisted war in the past.

Civil Disobedience

Many war resisters believe that laws which make war possible are immoral. They're willing to break the law to help bring about peace. Often on demonstrations, for instance, some of the demonstrators will cross police lines that they believe are wrong. From the 1950s to today, war resisters sometimes enter nuclear test sites and are arrested.

Most people who break the law in this way expect to be arrested. They take their stand as a way of showing the public that the laws they are breaking are wrong or wrongly applied. Civil disobedience has been used by labor unions, the independence movement in India, the civil rights movement of the 1960s, and the anti-nuclear-power movement in addition to the peace movement. For more information, check some of the books under "Further Reading" at the end of this book.

War Tax Resistance

One way to resist war is to refuse to pay for it. War tax resisters believe that it's wrong for them to pay taxes when over half of the federal budget goes for the military. They usually don't face jail because the Internal Revenue Service can get the taxes they owe, plus interest and penalties, by seizing their bank accounts or property.

War tax resistance and the tax laws are very complex. You shouldn't refuse to pay your taxes without talking to a good tax resistance counselor. CCCO can help you to find one if you decide you object to war taxes.

A Final Word

Whether you become a conscientious objector, and what that decision means for your life, is up to you. No one can decide for you, and no one can lead your life for you. But you're not alone. Thousands of others have faced these questions and made decisions similar to the ones you're making now. For many, becoming a CO was a turning point in their lives; others were not so powerfully affected. But nearly all COs found that they were changed in some way just by thinking about their stand on war and making a decision.

Deciding whether to be a conscientious objector isn't easy, particularly in a world where soldiers are well-respected and COs are often regarded as cowards and scorned as "shirkers." In fact, most COs are neither. They are part of a long tradition that has sought ways to end war and in which each person has begun with himself or herself. Whether you wish to join that tradition is between you and your conscience. In the process of deciding, you can learn a lot about war and peace— and about yourself.

Things to Think About

☞ Do you think the world is more or less dangerous now that they Cold War has ended?

☞ How important do you think it is to live by your values?

☞ If you could right one wrong in the world, what would it be?

☞ What do you think you can do to make a better world?

Ideas for Papers

✍ Do a study of the groups in your community that work for peace or social justice.

✍ Study one group in your community that works for peace or social justice. How did it start? What does it do? How does it get funding?

✍ Compile a listing of opportunities for volunteers in your community. Call some of the groups to see what volunteers actually do.

Chapter 13
You and Military Recruitment

If you're thinking about becoming a conscientious objector, you probably aren't interested in joining the military. Unless you go to a school that bans all military recruiters, though, chances are you've seen recruiters at work. Military recruiters regularly visit some high schools, while in others they set up exhibits on career days or give special presentations to student assemblies. And you've probably seen some of the thousands of military recruiting advertisements that appear on television and in magazines directed at young people.

You can't avoid making decisions about the military. The recruiting commands are working too hard to get your attention and persuade you to join. This chapter discusses why people enlist, how the military tries to recruit them, and how you can help your friends to protect themselves if they are thinking about enlisting. Even if you've already decided not to enlist, you should read this chapter because it talks about things that the recruiters *don't* tell you.

Why People Enlist

There are a lot of reasons why people decide to join the military—for example, because they feel they owe their country some service. But most people don't sign up for idealistic reasons like that one. Here are the four most common reasons why people enlist:

✔ *Unemployment:* Studies by the Department of Defense and independent economists show that the number and quality of people applying to enlist improve during hard times. This is particularly true among people of color because unemployment rates in their communities are often double the national rate or worse. If you can't find a job, the military looks like a good choice—or maybe the only choice you have.

✔ *Training and Education:* Military advertisements and recruiters promise training in job skills that you can use in civilian life after your discharge. With the cost of college very high and the cost of private vocational training high as well, the military can look like a good place to get a skill and start your career.

✔ *Educational and Other Benefits:* Both the ads and the recruiters often mention that you can "save money for college" while you complete your enlistment. Veterans can also qualify for other benefits, like special mortgages. These benefits can look very attractive for someone who wants to go to college or eventually buy a house, but doesn't have the money to do so.

✔ *Travel and Adventure:* With troops stationed all over the world, the military can and often does picture itself as a way of getting away from home and having an exciting experience. This can be particularly attractive to someone who wants to leave home anyway but doesn't have the means to do so.

Most people enlist for one or more of these reasons. Military claims about training, benefits, and travel all have some truth, but all are also very misleading. Anyone thinking about enlisting should look carefully at any claims or promises which his or her recruiter may make.

The Military Recruiting System

Each military branch has its own recruiting command, with its own recruiting budget. The national commands supervise regional commands, which are in turn responsible for local recruiting offices. To understand what recruiters actually do, you don't have to know all the details of the command structure. But knowing who is in charge is important if you're in the Delayed Entry Program (see below) and want to get a discharge.

Local recruiters have very little authority. They can't, for example, authorize a discharge from the Delayed Entry Program. And any promises they make are worthless unless they are written into the recruit's enlistment agreement.

A large part of the military recruiting budget goes into advertising—like the ads you may have seen on television when you watched a baseball game. These ads don't use actual military personnel, any more than ads portraying washing machine repairmen use actual repairmen. They use actors. They usually don't talk about the military's mission, which is to make war, but about the benefits of joining the military. Sometimes they don't tell the whole truth—as in ads about college benefits which don't tell you how little the modern GI Bill actually covers.

None of this is very surprising. The ads are trying to

sell the military. The recruiting commands and the ad agencies know that people are more likely to enlist to get money for college than to get training in infantry combat.

The recruiting commands do a lot of advertising, but the real work of recruiting is done by local recruiters—the people in uniform whom you may have seen in your school or neighborhood. Recruiters are salespeople. They spend a lot of time making contacts with "centers of influence"—people like guidance counselors who can recommend the military to potential recruits—and with young people. Each recruiter has an assigned quota of recruits per month. The military often reassigns recruiters who don't produce to less desirable military jobs. This puts a lot of pressure on the recruiter to make sure that his or her prospects actually enlist.

Local recruiters and recruiting commands use every common marketing tool, along with some that civilian salespeople don't have. Potential recruits, for example, often receive mailings from recruiting offices in each military branch. Recruiters visit malls and video arcades, give talks at high schools, visit with church youth groups—any place where they think they can reach young people. Even if you don't want to have anything to do with the military, you may at least get a mailing from a recruiting office or hear a recruiting presentation at your school.

As the military cut back in the early 1990s, the number of military recruiters did not decrease. As long as the military must recruit over a quarter of a million new people each year, it's unlikely to cut back significantly on recruiting.

The Enlistment Agreement

Suppose you decided to enlist, that you had passed the physical, mental and "moral" tests, and that the recruiter wanted to sign you up. What would you be signing, and what should you know about it?

When you enlist, you sign a military enlistment agreement. You can get a copy of the current agreement from CCCO if you're interested. The military calls this document an "agreement" rather than a "contract" because it isn't a contract as the law usually understands that word.

If you sign a contract to buy a car, the contract will usually say what you have to do (for instance, pay a certain amount of money) *and* what the auto dealer has to do (for instance, supply you with the car specified in the contract). If the dealer can't supply the car as agreed, the contract is off, and you don't have to pay. If you're unable to raise the money and haven't already taken delivery of the car, you can call off the deal too.

That's not how most military enlistment agreements work. In most of them, the military agrees to provide certain training or certain initial assignments or both *if you qualify.* If you don't qualify—or, in some cases, if the training is no longer available—your obligation to the military doesn't end. The military can then assign you as it wishes. In very rare instances, the enlistment agreement may require the military to discharge you if it can't deliver the training as promised. But such a promise would not protect you unless it was a specific, written provision of the enlistment agreement. If you don't have it in writing, the military can use you as it sees fit.

The enlistment agreement also doesn't require the

military to actually assign you to work in your field once you've completed your training. If military needs require it, the military can assign a trained computer expert to work in the kitchen. That wouldn't make a lot of sense, but it can happen. So there's no guarantee that you'll get experience in the work for which you trained.

All of this makes the military enlistment agreement very one-sided—so one-sided that it might not stand up under civilian contract law. The courts, however, don't apply civilian standards to military enlistment agreements. It's up to the recruit to make sure he or she knows what is in the agreement and what is not, and to make a careful decision about signing the agreement.

Military Training

The military has hundreds of job classifications or "Military Occupation Specialties" (MOS). Many of them involve skills that, in theory at least, would be useful in civilian life as well as the military. This is the basis for recruiting claims about job training.

Many people who enlist get the job training they sought, but many others don't—or find that the training isn't what they expected. There are at least two reasons for this:

✔ *The military's mission is making war, not providing job training.* This seems pretty obvious, but it isn't always clear to new recruits. Making war is not like running a business. A civilian business doesn't have to plan on having twenty or thirty percent of its personnel killed and wounded when it is doing its job. The military does. This means that military workers must be easy to replace—which in turn means that each military job has to be so specific that if the person doing it is killed, a replacement can move in and start performing right away, without extensive training. So the military divides tasks into smaller tasks and trains its workers to do the smaller tasks as part of a team.

The military's combat mission also affects what kinds of training may be available and how much use they might be in civilian life. Training as a combat infantry soldier, for example, has no use at all in civilian life, yet recruiters are always on the lookout for potential combat soldiers because combat is central to the military's mission. Many other military specialties, such as artillery maintenance and operating tanks, have little value in civilian life. Civilian corporations don't generally use artillery to do their jobs.

No matter what training a recruit gets, in time of war he or she may be assigned to a different field. The military can use all of its personnel as needed when there is a war. It can also do so in peacetime, but assignment to the wrong job is even more likely in wartime than in peacetime.

✔ *Military job classifications aren't always what they seem.* Because the military divides jobs into very specific and limited tasks, a military job specialty that looks attractive may not actually give you the broad experience you need for the civilian job market. A job with a title like "Motor Maintenance Specialist," for example, may really give you experience in changing the oil in a tank—and very little else. (The job title, by the way, is fictitious.)

Anyone who is thinking about enlisting for special training and a specific job title should be sure to find out what a person with that job title *actually does*. Potential recruits also should check whether they can get job training from a civilian agency before they consider the military. A local pre-enlistment or military counselor may be able to help. Contact CCCO for the name of someone near you.

Education and Other Benefits

For many years, military veterans benefited from the post-World War II GI Bill. The GI Bill paid for their education, helped them with loans and mortgages, and provided other benefits.

Today's GI Bill, known as the "Montgomery GI Bill" after its sponsor, Sen. Sonny Montgomery (D-MS), provides far fewer benefits than the older GI Bill. It is designed as a matching fund, which means that for every dollar you save toward college while you're in the military, the government adds a certain number of dollars. If you don't remain in the military long enough, you get no money for college. CCCO can send you a detailed pamphlet on the Montgomery GI Bill if you want more information.

The Montgomery GI Bill doesn't guarantee that the law won't change while you are in the military. Congress could decide to cut all veterans' educational benefits, and your enlistment agreement would not protect you. Though this is unlikely, budget cuts and loss of benefits have happened in the past. In the early 1980s, for example, Congress repealed a special enlistment bonus while most of the people who qualified for it were still in the military. These people never received the money they were promised when they enlisted.

Anyone who is considering enlistment to get money

for college should look at other alternatives first. Guidance counselors or college financial aid officers may be able to help. Or for information on alternatives to the GI Bill, contact CCCO or one of the groups listed at the back of this book.

Travel and Adventure

Military advertisements and recruiting leaflets often show nice-looking military personnel enjoying the sights of Europe or other exciting places. If you've never been outside the country, traveling abroad can be an exciting prospect.

The pictures in the brochures, however, are pretty misleading. The "military personnel" are usually models, and a recruit may never actually be assigned to Europe. Even worse, military pay, while better than it was twenty years ago, still hasn't kept up with inflation and the weak dollar in foreign countries. So that exciting tour may never happen because you can't afford it.

U.S. troops are stationed in many places around the world, so it's quite possible that if you enlist you might go overseas. But you would spend most of your time on a military base performing your duties. You might encounter problems with local people who don't like U.S. troops, have racist attitudes, or feel free to overcharge Americans. You might not speak the local language, and the military probably won't help you to learn it. Many soldiers find that an overseas deployment is a very unpleasant experience—not the "tour" that the brochures picture. Others make the most of their time, learn the local language and customs, and have good memories of their overseas assignment. But there are no guarantees.

Special Military Recruitment Programs

If you're in high school, there are two special military recruitment programs that you should know about. One is a military vocational test; the other is a military training program. This section discusses these programs, as well as state laws regarding recruitment that you should know about.

The Armed Services Vocational Aptitude Battery

The Armed Services Vocational Aptitude Battery (ASVAB) is a series of aptitude tests, strongly oriented toward potential for military performance. Many schools use it as a substitute for other, more comprehensive aptitude tests. Schools can use ASVAB without charge.

ASVAB's critics have pointed to its bias in favor of military-type skills—which isn't surprising, since it is a military test—and its bias against women. They have argued that ASVAB doesn't actually measure aptitude for civilian jobs. An even more serious issue, however, is ASVAB's use as a recruiting tool. It is administered by military personnel. Local recruiters receive a list of students who took the test, along with their scores and home addresses, so that they can contact people who look like good prospects for enlistment. Many critics believe that providing recruiters with a list of potential recruits is not the business of the schools.

If your school uses ASVAB, and you want to work on getting them to use a civilian test, contact CCCO or one of the groups listed in the back for help.

Junior Reserve Officers Training Corps (JROTC)

Many colleges around the U.S. offer training in the Reserve Officers Training Corps (ROTC). If you're in ROTC and want to get a discharge as a conscientious objector, you should get CCCO's book, *Advice for Conscientious Objectors in the Armed Forces,* and contact CCCO for the name of a military counselor near you.

Junior ROTC is a high school program. Joining and completing it doesn't give you officer status in the military. Those who have completed JROTC can qualify to enter the military at the rank of E-2 (private first class) instead of E-1 (private)—not a very big jump in rank. JROTC is entirely a military training and indoctrination program. Members of JROTC units wear uniforms, have classes in military subjects like military courtesy, and go through simple military drills. In some military branches, JROTC members receive weapons training at a nearby base.

JROTC's supporters argue that it trains young people in citizenship and gives them added discipline. Opponents argue that military training isn't appropriate for high school students, that JROTC costs money which hard-pressed school districts ought to be using for improving their regular programs, and that training students in violent solutions to problems isn't a good idea.

CCCO can provide more information about JROTC if you're interested. You'll have to decide for yourself what you think about military training in the high schools. Do you think it's a good use of school money and time? Do you think your school should be providing military training? If your answer to these questions is no,

CCCO and some of the other groups listed in the back of this book can help with information on how to organize against JROTC.

State Recruiting Laws

In a growing number of states, the law now requires local school districts to provide military recruiters with lists of high school seniors. Religious schools are usually exempt from these requirements, but public schools are not. Some states, such as Pennsylvania, allow students to request that their names not be sent to recruiters. For information on whether your state requires school districts to give lists of students to recruiters, contact CCCO or one of the groups listed at the back of this book.

The Delayed Entry Program

Probably the most-used military recruitment program is the Delayed Entry Program (DEP). People who enlist under the DEP sign up for the military. They are then placed in "inactive reserve" status and do not report for active duty until up to a year after they enlisted. While on delay, they are members of the military, but they have no official duties. Recruiters hold regular meetings with them and encourage them to bring their friends in to the recruiting office—to help the recruiter "sell" the military. If a person in the DEP wants to leave the military, he or she must apply for discharge; you cannot simply resign from the DEP.

If you or someone you know has joined the DEP and wants a discharge, CCCO's pamphlet, "If You Change Your Mind...A Guide to Discharge from the Delayed Entry Program," can help. Contact CCCO or one of the groups listed at the back of this book.

Equal Opportunity?

Military advertisements often portray the military as a place of equal opportunity for people of color and women. Many people accept this image, but it is very misleading. This section briefly discusses the problems of people of color and women in the military. For more information, consult some of the books listed under "Further Reading," at the back of this book.

People of Color

Facing unemployments rates that are sometimes double the rates in the white community, people of color often find the military a relatively attractive prospect. As of October, 1991, 29.72% of military personnel were persons of color.

The military provides employment for people of color, but, despite its image, it does poorly in providing opportunities for advancement. Only 12.79% of the officer corps were persons of color—far fewer than you would expect if the military really provided the opportunities the public thinks.

These figures are only one example. A very high percentage of low-level combat jobs (for instance, ordinary front-line infantry) are filled by persons of color—far more than you would expect if military opportunities were fairly distributed. These jobs are least likely to provide training and experience in skills for the civilian job market. Persons of color receive a disproportionate number of less-than-honorable discharges, which can cause serious problems finding a civilian job. In many ways the military is a reflection of the civilian world, where persons of color are still struggling for full equality. Because soldiers are required to follow orders and because once you're in the military you can't just quit, racial problems in the military may sometimes be even more difficult than they are in civilian life.

Although they get little publicity, racial incidents do occur in the military. A few military people are even members of the Ku Klux Klan. Incidents like these are not common, but the military is by no means free of them.

If you're thinking about enlisting because the military provides equal opportunity, check things out carefully before you decide. That way you may avoid some very unpleasant surprises.

Women

Women are an important part of the military. Military commanders lavished praise on women's performance during the Persian Gulf War (1991) and the U.S. invasion of Panama (1989).

The achievements of women in the military come at a price. For thousands of years, war and the military were essentially all-male institutions. Women were not welcome. Today, women's prospects for promotion in the military are limited because, except for some jobs in the Navy, they can only perform "non-combat" jobs, and women in the military face high rates of rape and sexual harassment.

You may oppose all wars and may not think it's very important whether the military assigns women to combat jobs. But a "combat" job in the military doesn't always involve hiding in a foxhole. It can be a desirable command slot or a very good military job for an enlisted person—and women need not apply. The rules against assigning women to combat jobs are a form of discrimination, whatever the reasons the military gives for them.

Rape and sexual harassment are common in civilian life as well as in the military. But traditional military attitudes toward women—which assume that women in the military are more sexually available than civilian women—have been very slow to change. Making the problem worse is the fact that soldiers are trained in violence, and this often affects their behavior toward women (and other men, for that matter).

If you or a woman you know are thinking of enlisting, take the time to learn more about the problems of women in the military. CCCO and the groups listed at the back of this book can provide more information.

Homosexuals in the Military

Gay men and lesbians are eligible for military enlistment, but any military member who states that he or she is gay will be discharged. Homosexual acts and same-sex marriages are violations of military law and can lead to court-martial. If a homosexual states publicly that he or she is gay but does not admit to gay sex acts while in the military, he or she will receive a discharge under honorable conditions.

This policy, called "Don't Ask, Don't Tell," was an unsatisfactory compromise between ending the gay ban completely and retaining it completely. Immediately after his election in 1992, President Bill Clinton moved to end the military's ban on gay people. Because of opposition from the Congress and the Joint Chiefs of

Staff, he could not simply lift the ban. The military agreed not to ask recruits whether they were gay, but openly gay people were still subject to involuntary discharge. How this policy will work in practice remained unclear when this book was written.

If you're gay and want to enlist, keep in mind that even though you can now enlist (if you keep quiet about your sexual preference), the military will continue to be a hostile place for gays. Military tradition in the U.S. is strongly anti-gay, and it will take years to overcome the prejudices of the military establishment. You'll have to decide for yourself whether enlistment is for you.

If you want more information about the problems of gay people in the military, or an update on the status of the gay ban, contact one or more of the groups listed in the back of this book.

Protecting Yourself and Your Friends

If you're thinking of enlisting or know someone who is, there are some simple precautions you can take to make sure you don't make a mistake.

✔ *Don't talk with the recruiter alone.* Take someone with you as a witness.

✔ *Never give false information to the recruiter.* If a recruiter asks you to falsify information about your record or any other matter, say no. Falsifying information in order to enlist is a crime under military law, and if you're court-martialed it will be your word against that of the recruiter.

✔ *Don't sign any documents until you've taken them home and studied them.* This would apply to any legal transaction, but it's doubly important with military enlistment documents.

✔ *Keep copies of all documents.* Again, this applies to any legal transaction.

✔ *Accept no oral promises.* Remember, if what the recruiter promised isn't in your written agreement, it is worthless.

✔ *Talk with people who have been in the military before you decide.* Some people had a good experience; others had a bad one. Try to find people who had both.

Equal Access to Your School

If there are recruiters in your school, you may think the school should give equal time to people speaking for peace. The courts agree with you. As long as your school provides recruiters with a "forum," it must also open its doors to people with a different point of view. It can't keep them out because it disagrees with their position. Students and peace groups in many communities like Atlanta and Chicago have developed programs to get information on alternatives to enlistment into their schools.

Even with the law on your side, getting peace information into your school may require a lot of work. If you're interested in working on this issue, contact CCCO or one of the groups listed at the back of this book for details.

Things to Think About

☞ Do you know anybody who has enlisted in the military? Why did he or she enlist?

☞ Has anybody in your family been in the military? What happened to them?

☞ What do you think is the reason most people enlist?

☞ Do you think you have a duty to serve your country? What ways can you think of to do this?

Ideas for Papers

✍ Visit a recruiting station and talk with the recruiters about how they work. Then talk with a sales representative for a civilian business. Compare the two conversations.

✍ Do a survey of recruiters and the military at your school, including visits by recruiters, Junior ROTC, and ASVAB.

✍ Write a proposal to bring a speaker on peace to your school. Include background on the law, information on the military at your school, and a brief discussion of what the speaker might present.

Chapter 14
Is There a Draft in Your Future?

If you're a man who might be subject to a future military draft, you're probably wondering how likely such a draft might be and how it might come about. This chapter discusses different proposals for reinstating conscription (another name for the draft) and the reasons why some people oppose conscription.

Status of the Draft Law

The legal authority for the draft and the Selective Service System is the Military Selective Service Act as revised in 1971. Unless Congress actually repeals this law, it will remain on the books even when there is no active draft. The President can require men subject to the draft law to register with Selective Service, but he or she cannot reinstate inductions (orders to report for military duty) without authority from Congress.

The Standby Draft

The Military Selective Service Act says that if inductions end, the draft system is to remain in "standby" status. When the law was written, many in Congress thought this meant that people would be registered, classified, and perhaps even given physical examinations. It hasn't worked out that way. From 1972 to 1974, people were required to register, and local boards did actually classify them. Registration was suspended in 1975, but a new registration was proclaimed in July, 1980.

The idea behind the standby draft is to keep a "pool" of possible draftees ready for an emergency. But it's not clear what would be an "emergency," or whether such a crisis is likely. For a further discussion of the mobilization draft, see the next section of this chapter and "The Mobilization Draft" in the Appendix to this book.

Mobilization and the Draft

For many years, U.S. military plans focused on countering a massive attack in Europe by the forces of the Warsaw Pact. In a full-scale conventional war between the two superpowers and their allies, half a million or more soldiers on each side might have been killed and wounded in the first six weeks of fighting. The draft was supposed to provide replacements after the U.S. had used up both active-duty combat troops and combat Reservists. The mobilization draft was designed to provide replacements quickly. Critics of the mobilization draft argued that a full-scale European war was likely to become a nuclear war very quickly, and in a nuclear war the draft would be irrelevant.

With the end of the Warsaw Pact in 1990, a full-scale mobilization became very unlikely, and a return to the mobilization draft also became unlikely. Plans for mobilization, however, remain in place.

How the Draft Might Return

If the mobilization draft is unlikely, what is the danger of a return to the draft? Nobody really knows, but there are several ways that the draft might return in some form. Here are a few of them:

Long but "Low-Level" War

It's possible that the U.S. might become involved in a long war which, though not as large as a full-scale European war, could lead to calls for a new draft. Had the U.S. sent ground troops to Bosnia in 1992, for example, those forces might have found that they could not quickly defeat their adversaries and go home. Withdrawing troops once a nation has committed them can be very difficult. Intervention in Bosnia in 1992 might therefore have led to a long war which would, over time, use large numbers of combat troops.

A new draft for a long, "low-level" war might not look very much like the draft described in the Appendix. Even if Congress reinstated the draft without change, their decision would probably only happen after a lot of debate not only about the draft but about the war, foreign policy, and other issues. During the debate, opponents of the draft would be able to organize and possibly even block it.

Recruiting Shortfalls

In the early years after the end of inductions, military recruiters did not sign up all the recruits they were supposed to. Called a "shortfall," this lack of new recruits led to calls for a new draft (or some other form of conscription) throughout the 1970s.

Today's military is smaller than the military of the 1970s, but recruiting it can still be difficult. During the early 1990s, when U.S. forces were being cut, many recruiters complained that they had problems convincing potential recruits to consider enlisting. Some military planners worried that the military wouldn't be able to attract good-quality recruits.

Whenever the military has recruiting problems, some in Congress and other places may call for a new draft. Because reinstating the draft would be unpopular, most Congress members would probably not listen to these calls. They might, for example, appropriate more money for recruiting. But a new draft to fill recruiting shortfalls could happen. Such a draft would probably be different from the mobilization draft. It might look more like a "national service" program, as described in the next section.

National Service

The most popular alternative to the all-volunteer military, and one which could easily come about, is "national service." There are actually four types of national service proposals. You'll have to decide for yourself whether you can support any of them:

✔ *Small-Scale Voluntary Programs:* In a small-scale voluntary program, the federal government would either directly hire or provide funding for volunteers who would work for a special government agency or would be assigned to community groups. Such a program might hire or fund anywhere from a few hundred to several hundred thousand volunteers. Participants in the program might receive special benefits like additional student aid upon completion of their service, but no one would be penalized for not taking part.

An example of a small-scale national service program is the Peace Corps, which sends a small number of volunteers to do community and technical work in countries which request them. Other proposals would give funding directly to community groups or would allow national service participants to postpone repayment of student loans while volunteering.

✔ *Large-Scale Voluntary:* Under a large-scale voluntary service program, the Federal government would hire or fund not thousands but millions of volunteers. Jobs might be provided by a federal national service agency, by local groups or by some combination of the two. Participants would earn credit toward benefits by taking part in national service, but those who chose not to do so could still obtain benefits.

Military enlistment would be one choice under most large-scale voluntary national service proposals. Those who enlisted might earn more benefits than those who chose civilian work.

✔ *Large-Scale Semi-Voluntary:* Under a slightly different type of proposal, *only* those who took part in national service would qualify for benefits. This would put a great deal of pressure on potential volunteers. For many, national service participation would in effect be required if they needed money to go to college, needed federal job training, or needed other federal benefits.

Military enlistment would be one choice under all large-scale semi-voluntary national service proposals. Those who enlisted might earn more benefits than those who chose civilian work.

✔ *Large-scale Involuntary:* Under a large-scale involuntary program, every person of military age would be required to perform either military duty or civilian work with the federal government or a community group. National service workers would earn credit toward federal benefits, but even those in civilian work would have to complete a specified term of service or face legal penalties. Those who chose military duty might earn more benefits than those who chose civilian work.

Thinking About National Service

Many people find national service proposals attractive. Those who support them say that they would help rebuild our society by providing volunteer workers. Under an involuntary program, COs would not have to apply for conscientious objector status; they could simply choose civilian work—as could many others who do not wish to take part in war but don't qualify for CO status under current law. Supporters of large-scale programs also argue that national service would help military recruiting.

There's little doubt that many community and nonprofit groups would benefit from additional volunteers. What's not so clear is whether a national service program, especially a large-scale involuntary one, is the best way to provide such help. A large-scale program that required everyone to participate would have to find jobs for up to four million young people each year. This could prove very difficult, and if the federal government funded national service participants rather than just finding jobs with private groups, it could also be very expensive.

Critics of required national service argue that forcing people to do civilian work may be unconstitutional, that such a program wouldn't work, and that it would interfere with participants' freedom. What do you think?

What's Wrong with the Draft?

Since 1973, the U.S. has had no legal conscription. The change to an all-volunteer military began because the Vietnam War draft was unpopular, but there were other reasons why people opposed conscription (and draft registration). Here are some of them:

✔ Registration for the draft gives the government a list of names of young people which it otherwise might not have. This could lead to abuses. To enforce registration, for example, the Selective Service System uses a system of computer checks which the government would not do if there were no registration.

✔ The draft interferes with people's lives. It not only forces people into the military, but those who don't enter the military may change their school or career plans because of the draft. If you're a CO and the draft system doesn't recognize your claim, you may even face prison.

✔ The draft makes it easier for the government to go to war. Expanding the military, even for an unpopular war, is easier with the draft. If there had been no draft, for example, the government would have had a much harder time recruiting troops for the Vietnam War, and the war might have ended more quickly.

✔ The draft costs human lives. Although good generals try to conserve the lives of their troops, the fact that a commander can obtain replacement troops easily may lead to wars of "attrition," in which both sides sustain many killed and wounded until one side or the other gives up from sheer exhaustion.

Making Choices and Protecting Yourself

It's unlikely that the U.S. will reinstate conscription without some warning. Even in the era of modern, fast-moving warfare, a conflict large enough to lead to full mobilization would not happen without at least some preliminary fighting or international incidents. Modern armies can move quickly when they attack, but it is almost impossible to conceal a major military buildup—which would come before even the most rapid "surprise attack"—from intelligence satellites.

Although you would have at least some warning in the event of mobilization, it's a good idea to plan ahead, following the suggestions in Chapter 2, to protect yourself.

If conscription should return in some other form, such as compulsory national service, you'll have plenty of warning, and you will have a contribution to make to the debate. Because you would be affected by any new conscription law, your point of view should carry special weight with your Congress member. You'll need to think about what kinds of national service, if any, you can accept and what kinds you reject. You need to think about how conscription in the U.S. would affect not only you but people you know, your community, the nation as a whole, and the rest of the world. And you need to think about how best to act on your beliefs.

These are difficult issues, but they could be important for your life and the lives of many others. If you'd like to learn more about them, contact CCCO or one of the groups listed under "Some Groups That Work for Peace," in the Appendix to this book.

Things to Think About

☞ Do you think the U.S. might again use the draft some day? If so, how do you think this might happen?

☞ What do you think about national service? Would you be willing to be part of it? Do you think it would work? What kind(s) of national service, if any, do you support?

☞ Do you agree with the arguments against conscription in this chapter? Why or why not?

Ideas for Papers

✍ Write a brief history of how the active draft ended in the early 1970s.

✍ Write a brief history of how draft registration was reinstated in 1980.

Chapter 15
A Note to Parents and Grandparents

As I write this chapter, my own daughter is just finishing ninth grade. She is 15, a little younger than most of her class. Like many 15-year-olds, she has a strong sense of right and wrong, and she thinks long and carefully about moral decisions. Like her mom and dad, she is strongly committed to peace, but she knows that her family would support her no matter what her position on war. We are happy that she has reached her own conclusions on this difficult issue, and we are proud of her for doing so.

My daughter is not alone. Many young people of all ages worry about war and how it might affect them. This chapter is one parent's reflections on how to help your son(s) or daughter(s) to think about these issues. For convenience, I will use the term "your child," even though I may be talking about people like my daughter who are long out of childhood. The suggestions in this chapter may also help grandparents who want to guide their grandchildren through decisions about war.

Talking about war with your child isn't quite like discussing drugs or sex. It can be far less personal. But the values which your child must form and the decisions he or she must make about war can be very personal indeed. Your help and support can mean the difference between a well-thought-out and a hasty decision about the military—and that decision can be and often is a life-and-death matter.

Setting Your Own Goal

As you help your child to think about war, you need to make some of your own choices. What, for example, is your own position on war? If you're reading this chapter, you're probably committed to the search for peace, but what does this mean in your life? Does it affect your choice of job, your spare-time activities, your decisions on whether to pay taxes, or other decisions?

Being committed to peace does *not* mean living in any particular way, but if you do feel moved to live out your commitment in some way, your example may help your child to think about what peace means for him or her. You may find it helpful to read this book, either along with your child, or on your own. You'll also find the readings under "A Short Course on War and Peace," in the Appendix, helpful.

You also need to think about why you want your child to think about war. Do you want to teach him or her a certain set of values? Many parents do. My own goal in talking with my daughter has been to help her make well-thought-out decisions, not to teach her what decisions to make; but that is *my* choice. What is yours?

How would you feel if your child joined the military? In my years of counseling, I have encountered many families that have literally split apart when one son became a conscientious objector or a daughter joined the Air Force. By thinking in advance about this issue, you may prevent hard feelings later on.

Peace at an Early Age

It is never too early to start helping your child to think about peace. You can't, of course, expect a five-year-old child to cope with the same complex issues that a grown child could. But children's habits and attitudes about violence, racial equality, and a host of other important issues, begin to develop very early.

In the list of readings at the end of this book, you will find material on non-violence and children. Look at it to see whether it meets your needs. If you're a member of a church, find out what your church teaches about war and whether it has any materials for young children. You might also find it helpful to learn about the phases of moral development. *Raising Good Children,* by Thomas Lickona, PhD (New York: Bantam Books, 1983) is an excellent place to begin.

Avoid speaking for your children or taking actions on their behalf. For example, a CCCO Conscientious Objector Card (see Chapter 18) prepared by a parent for a five-year-old has little value. Your child can decide whether or not to register with CCCO when he or she is old enough to understand the significance of doing so.

Peace in the Early Teens

By age 12 or 13, your child may have begun to think about war—or may not. Here are some ways you can encourage him or her to do so. Many of these suggestions also apply to military-age young people.

✔ *Keep informed yourself.* Throughout this book, I have suggested that keeping informed is the first step in choosing peace. That also applies to parents.

✔ *If possible, have family meals together.* This sounds like a simple step, but families who do not have meals together miss chances to talk and learn from each other. My daughter learned much of what she knows about the military by taking part in dinner conversation.

✔ *Watch films or videos about war and peace together.* There are many excellent feature films on war. The best of them present moral questions in a graphic form which can lead to some very enlightening discussions.

✔ *Encourage your child's school to include material on war and peace in its curriculum.* Although some schools worry that such material will be "controversial," others may be eager to include it with a little prodding.

Peace at Military Age

By age 16 or 17, your child may be hearing from military recruiters or seeing them in school. He or she will need help to make a good decision. You can provide it. Here are some suggestions:

✔ *Don't impose your own values.* You probably already know that this won't work and could lead your child to reject values which he or she might otherwise accept. If you make your own stand clear and live consistently with it, you've done what is most important.

✔ *Suggest that your child read this book and other peace-oriented material if he or she wishes to do so.*

✔ *Make clear to your child that you will support him or her even if you disagree with his or her decision.* And be sure that you make good on this promise.

✔ *Learn about military recruitment, either from this book or from other materials available from CCCO.* The more you know, the better you can help if your child seeks your advice.

✔ *Make sure you know how to get help if your child needs it.* The simplest way to get help is to call CCCO for the name of a counselor near you.

A Final Word

Helping your child to make good choices about the military is not easy, but there is nothing mysterious or abstruse about it. Most of the suggestions in this chapter are based on common sense. If you know where you yourself stand, keep informed about war and peace, and talk about these issues with your child, you will be doing what you can. The rest is up to your child—with your support.

—*Robert A. Seeley*

Things to Think About

☞ What did you do about the military? Would you do the same again?

☞ Why do you want your child to think about war and conscience?

☞ How would you feel if your child joined the military? If he or she became a conscientious objector?

☞ What difference do your convictions make in your life now?

Part V

About the Draft...

Chapter 16
Registration—Your Decision

If you're a man eighteen or nearing that age, you'll have to decide whether or not to register with the Selective Service System. Men registered with Selective Service could be included in a future draft. (For more on the draft, see Chapter 14 and Appendix I of this book.) Women aren't included under the current draft law, but Congress could change that at any time. Man or woman, it's best for you to think now about registration and what it means for you. This chapter explains what's involved, the most likely consequences, and why some people have resisted. It also gives guidelines that may help you think through your own stand. For more on what could—but probably won't—happen if you refuse to register, see Chapter 17.

The Law on Registration

The Military Selective Service Act requires male U.S. citizens aged 18 through 26 to register with Selective Service when the President orders them to do so. Many foreign citizens who live in the U.S. are also required to register.

The President can proclaim registration days by Executive Order if he thinks that a draft registration is needed. Or he can set up a "continuing" registration. An example of the first was the two-week registration held in July, 1980, for men born in 1960 and 1961. An example of the second was the registration requirement in effect from 1948 to 1974, when all men were required to register at the time they reached 18.

At present, all men are required to register with Selective Service within a sixty-day period that begins thirty days before their 18th birthdays—that is, within thirty days before or twenty-nine days after their 18th birthdays.

Registration can be held whether or not inductions are taking place. For instance, no inductions are taking place now, but men are still required to register.

WARNING: The details on registration, who must register, when they must register, etc., can change quickly. Do not rely on this chapter alone. Consult CCCO or your draft counselor for the latest information.

Registration Procedures

If you're included among those who must register, you'll be required to go to the Post Office and fill in a Registration Form (SSS Form 3). A copy of this form will be found at the end of this book.

Once you've filled in the Registration Form, a postal clerk will check to see that it's legible and then forward it to Selective Service. Your name will then be placed on Selective Service's computer listing of registrants for your year of birth.

WARNING: The Postal Service often loses mail. To protect yourself, make a copy of your completed Registration Form. Keep copies of everything you send to Selective Service.

Sometime after you register, Selective Service will send you a Registration Acknowledgement (SSS Form 3A). This form lets them check to see that they have correct information on you. If their information is correct, you don't have to return the attached form (SSS Form 3-B). You may want to do so, however, following the procedure suggested under "Your Choices," below.

Filling Out the Registration Form

The Registration Form asks for your name, address, date of birth, and Social Security Number. If you're unsure on any point, or if you still haven't decided whether you want to register, you have a legal right to take the form home and study it or discuss it with your draft counselor.

If you register, the Selective Service System can send your name to a military recruiter whether you want them to or not. You can't stop them from doing this, but you can write a note on the Registration Form saying that you object to having your name sent to a recruiter.

WARNING: Postal clerks sometimes tell registrants that they have no right to take the Registration Form home. This is not true. If you run into any problem, call CCCO or your draft counselor for help.

The instructions on the Registration Form and the Registration Acknowledgement say that you must fill in all the information requested, including your Social Security Number. If you object to giving Selective Service your Social Security Number, call CCCO or your draft counselor before you register to get information and ideas on how to protect yourself. The courts have ruled that Selective Service can require you to give your Social Security Number.

Selective Service does not now issue registration or classification cards, so your own record of the Registration Form and the Registration Acknowledgement may be the only proof you'll have that you registered. You can, however, ask the Director of Selective Service for evidence of your registration once every six months.

Your Choices

If you are required to register with Selective Service, you have six choices:

✔ *You can refuse to register and tell Selective Service, the President, the newspapers, etc., thus taking a public stand.* This action violates the Selective Service law. It increases your chances of facing prosecution. But you may want to do it to make a point about registration and the draft. In the past, thousands of people have publicly refused to register with just this idea in mind.

✔ *You can refuse to register and tell no one.* This "private" resistance also violates the law. But you're not as likely to be prosecuted as you would be if you took a public stand. If you object to registering but don't feel you want to make a public witness about it, this position may be the right one for you. Or you may simply feel that the government has no right to arrest you, and you don't have to help them. Either way, you shouldn't decide not to register because you don't think you'll be caught. Always think first about the worst that could happen, and whether you could face it, before you break the law.

If you resist in this way, you may want to write a statement of your reasons and place it in your personal file (see Chapter 18) in case you are prosecuted in the future.

✔ *You can register under protest.* Some peace groups have stickers which you can attach to your registration form, or you can just write your protest in the margin of the Registration Form. This position is legal. Selective Service will ignore your protest, but you will at least be on record against registration and the draft. Stickers can be peeled off, so you're safest writing your protest in the margin of the card.

✔ *You can try to let Selective Service know that you are a conscientious objector.* Again, some peace groups have stickers which you can attach to your registration form, or you can just write your claim in the margin and make a copy of your card for your records. It is legal to register as a conscientious objector. A simple statement like, "I am a conscientious objector to war in any form" is best. Selective Service will not process your claim or even acknowledge it. But you'll at least be on record. Again, keep in mind that stickers can be peeled off the Registration Form.

✔ *You can simply register, leaving your CO application— or your decision on whether you want to file an application— for later.* You can't hurt a later CO claim by doing this. As you can see by reading the Appendix on the mobilization draft, Selective Service rules don't even allow you to file for conscientious objector status until you're called for induction. Selective Service officials can't deny your claim because you followed the rules they themselves set up. It's important, however, for you to decide whether you're a CO. And if you ever have to file a CO claim, you can strengthen it if you begin gathering supporting evidence as soon as you can.

✔*You can register and make a CO statement with your Registration Acknowledgement.* When you receive your Registration Acknowledgement, you can return it, certified mail, return receipt requested, with a brief statement of your objection to war. Selective Service won't process this claim. Instead, they'll probably return it to you. But you'll still have a record that you tried to file. This could help a later claim.

After Registration

If you decide to resist after you've registered, there isn't much you can do to get your name off the Selective Service computer list. Resisters in the past have returned their draft cards, refused to fill out forms that Selective Service sent them, etc. You could refuse to return the Registration Acknowledgement, but if you do, Selective Service will merely assume that your address is correct. If you decide to resist after you've registered, you may not be able to do so until inductions begin again. But you can go on record against the draft by sending back your Registration Acknowledgement with a statement of protest. And if you're called for induction, you can refuse induction.

No registration cards will be issued under current procedures. So, if you want to resist, you can't send your cards back to Selective Service. You won't have any to send back.

The "Solomon Amendments"

When you're deciding whether to violate the law, you should always think about whether your conscience requires you to go to prison. You'll find more on this possibility in Chapter 17. But you probably won't face either court or prison because the government hasn't prosecuted many non-registrants. Instead, it has relied on the so-called "Solomon Amendments" (named after their sponsor, Rep. Gerald Solomon of New York) to pressure people to register.

The "Solomon Amendments" say that if you haven't registered with Selective Service as required you can't qualify for many Federal benefits. If you need Federal aid for college, for instance, you can't get it unless you have registered. And a non-registrant can't qualify for most Federal jobs. Many states also have Solomon-type restrictions on student aid, admission to state colleges, or other state benefits.

The Solomon Amendments can make your decision about registering more difficult. If your conscience tells you not to register, but you need Federal aid for college, you may find that there is no easy or good choice. For help in deciding and for information on alternatives to Federal aid, contact CCCO or one of the groups listed at the back of this book.

If You're Over 26

Until you reach your 26th birthday, you can change your mind about refusing to register at any time, and you probably won't face any penalties. But as this book went to press, Selective Service was refusing to accept registrations from men 26 and older. So if you reach age 26 and haven't registered, you may be permanently disqualified from Federal benefits covered by the Solomon Amendments.

This policy doesn't seem very fair, but it is a reality that you need to know about to make a good decision. If you decide to register, you can't wait indefinitely. You have to do it before you turn 26. And that means you have to make a decision before that day.

Why Some People Refuse to Register

This book can't tell you whether you should be a conscientious objector or refuse to register with Selective Service. You'll have to live with your decision, so you must, and should, decide for yourself what to do. But in the past, people have refused the draft for many reasons.

Nearly all draft resisters object to war. Their views on war aren't that much different from the views of people who apply for legal conscientious objector status—if they're different at all. But resisters often see the draft as part of the war system and believe it's important for them to refuse any kind of support for war that they can.

Some draft resisters object to conscription itself. They believe the government shouldn't have the right to draft people. In England during the Second World War there were even resisters who supported the war but felt it should be fought with volunteers. You can object to conscription and war all at once, of course, and most resisters do.

One reason for objecting to the draft is because it discriminates against the poor, minorities, and those with less education. This is certainly true. If you read over the chapters on conscientious objector status, you'll see that the draft rules favor people who read and write well. Even if you don't read and write well you can apply for and get CO status. But many people simply give up. Or they don't know they can apply. Minority people have less chance than others in our society to get a good education or a good job. And when there's a war, the people who have had fewer civilian opportunities often end up in the front lines.

Some resisters think that, by taking conscientious objector status, they would simply be helping the system to operate. They would be opening up a place for someone else to be drafted. Again, this is true enough. Unless the U.S. disbands its military or cuts back on defense, the military will get the people it needs, come what may. If there's a draft, it will get them by drafting them. And if there are a lot of COs, draft quotas will probably increase.

Finally, some resisters don't qualify for conscientious objector status at all. This is true, for instance, of people who object to only one war, such as Vietnam or the Persian Gulf War. If you don't object to all wars, you may decide to resist the draft. Or you could follow the suggestions in Chapter 18 and make your CO claim anyway. Either way, you may find that your conscience leads you to break the law—either by refusing to register or by refusing induction. But don't assume that you don't qualify for CO status until you've read the rest of this book.

None of this means that you should resist. There are good reasons for refusing to register, but there are also good reasons for deciding to register. What you do will depend on your values, your situation, your feelings about what you're ready to face, and many other factors.

Thinking About Registration

No one but you can decide whether you should register or refuse to do so. Here are some guidelines to help you think about your position:

✔ *Think about yourself.* What do you need to do to live with your conscience? If you resist, do you think you could face jail? What are your most important values?

✔ *Think about others.* There's nothing wrong or unusual about being concerned with your family. How would your resistance affect them? If you're married, how would it affect your marriage? Your children? Do you think it's worth the risk? Many do; others don't. Neither position is "wrong."

✔ *There is no one right position.* Many people have resisted the draft; many others have not. Often their views on war were pretty much the same. Resisters aren't "better" than people who decide to apply for CO status. And you won't be "worse," whichever road you take.

✔ *No one can be perfect.* Living in modern society is a compromise. If you resist the draft, you may still find that resisting taxes is not for you. And even if you resist the draft and the income tax, you may still pay federal taxes on gasoline—which support a highway system designed partly to help troop movements. You can't really avoid contributing to the military in some way. What you can do is decide in which ways you definitely *won't* contribute.

✔ *Talk about your position.* It's a good idea to talk with several people as you decide what to do. Talk with people who support resistance, with people who are against it, with your family, and with your draft counselor. You have to make your own choice, but other people can sometimes help you to see things more clearly.

✔*Don't be afraid to follow the law.* There's nothing "wrong" about following the law, and you don't need to feel guilty if that's your decision. Many people who object to war do register for the draft and apply for conscientious objector status. Sometimes people who support resistance will tell you this is a "cop-out," but it isn't. It's another way of expressing beliefs about war which are much the same as those of resisters. And there may be good reasons—like your family situation—why you shouldn't resist.

✔*Don't be afraid to resist.* If you decide to break the law, you'll have plenty of support. You can get help from the peace movement, from your friends, from your family, and from CCCO. If you're a member of a church, your church or minister will probably respect your conscience and help you. Even if you end in prison, you can get visits from your family and from Prisoner Visitation and Support Committee (for more information on PVS, contact CCCO).

The choice on whether to register is yours. Before you make it, you should read the rest of this book. You'll find it helpful to know just what's involved in legal conscientious objection, and some of the other chapters will help you to think about war, court, and prison. To resist or not to resist is a decision you shouldn't make without a lot of thought. The rest of this book, and the books under "Further Reading, " can give you a start.

Things to Think About

☞ If you're subject to Selective Service registration, what will you do about it? Have you registered? Refused to register? Why did you choose whichever you chose?

☞ Do you think it's fair to register men only?

Ideas for Papers

✍ How did today's draft registration come about? What was its stated purpose? Evaluate whether it really achieved that purpose.

Chapter 17
If You Break the Law...

When you think about whether to register, chances are your first question is whether the government can charge you with a crime and send you to prison. The answer to this question is theoretically yes, but since 1980, when draft registration was reinstated, the government has prosecuted fewer than 25 of the hundreds of thousands of non-registrants it could have charged. The threat resisters face now are loss of eligibility for financial aid for college, federal employment, and federal job training. For more information, see "The 'Solomon Amendments'" in Chapter 16.

This chapter talks about the worst that the government could do to you if you refuse to register and how unlikely that is to happen. It also discusses the series of "warning letters" that Selective Service sends to non-registrants. The "warning letters" are designed to frighten you into registering. They spell out the maximum penalty provided by law without explaining how unlikely it is that you will ever face trial, imprisonment, and fine. This chapter should help you to base your decision on a more balanced understanding of the facts.

Can You Go to Prison?

Refusing to register with Selective Service is a federal crime. So are refusing to report a change of address or other "minor" violations. They are felonies. Nonetheless, the chances that the government will prosecute you are slim. No one has gone to prison for a draft violation since 1987. If the government prosecutes you and you are convicted, you could be punished with up to five years in federal prison or up to $250,000 fine or both. But the government isn't likely to go after you for refusing to register, much less for "minor" Selective Service violations.

Many people want to know their chances of being indicted, convicted, or imprisoned. No one really knows in any particular case. During the Vietnam era, there were about 570,000 *reported* draft violators and many more who went undetected. Of these, 8750 were convicted; 3,250 of these men were sent to prison, and 5,500 of them were sentenced to probation or suspended sentence. For those who went to prison, the average sentence was less than three years, and few, if any, draft violaters spent more than two years behind bars.

Today, according to Selective Service, there are over 600,000 non-registrants, not counting late registrants. More than 330,000 of them have been reported to the Justice Department as "suspected violators." As of December, 1994, however, only 22 men have been indicted. Fifteen were convicted, and of these, seven were sentenced to prison. Time served in each case has been under seven months. There have been no new prosecutions since 1987.

The Justice Department couldn't prosecute all non-registrants even if it wanted to. It doesn't have the staff or the money. So, even though you should know what could happen to you if you were charged, the chances that you will be are very slight.

Federal Sentencing Guidelines

Federal sentencing guidelines provide for 0-6 month sentences and fines from $500.00 to $5,000.00 for non-registrants with no prior criminal records. A judge may also sentence a non-registrant to probation. People sentenced under the guidelines serve the actual time to which they are sentenced—less credit given for good behavior in prison—if the sentence is over a year. A sentence of less than a year may also be served in a halfway house.

WARNING: The guidelines described above apply only during periods when no one is actually being drafted. Sentencing guidelines during periods of active inductions are somewhat harsher. If inductions should begin again, contact CCCO or your draft counselor for the latest information.

Reminder Letters

If you haven't registered, you may receive several reminder letters. If you get a reminder letter and then register, you'll probably be safe. Selective Service has sent two types of reminder letters:

✔ Postcards: Sent to commercial lists of young men whether or not they have registered. Draft officials plan no followup.

✔ "Warning" Letters: Selective Service has bought lists of drivers, students, and other draft-age people from the states and other sources. Using these lists, they have now mailed hundreds of thousands of letters to "suspected non-registrants." Warning letters are sent in an envelope with a Selective Service return address and are signed by the Director of Selective Service. The first of these letters states that the law requires you to register and that you are subject to punishment if you don't. The second states that your name will be reported to the Justice Department if you don't register. The third states that your name has been reported for possible investigation. Occasionally the letters don't come in this exact order, and in some cases you may receive a fourth or even a fifth warning letter.

A warning letter does not mean you'll be prosecuted. It doesn't even mean that you will be investigated. If you don't respond to the first three warning letters, Selective Service may send your name to the Justice Department. Out of the hundreds of thousands of names sent to them, the Justice Department has investigated a few. For most, nothing has happened.

U.S. Attorneys have little or no interest in draft cases. In the unlikely event that the U.S. Attorney does decide to charge you, he or she may send you a warning letter by registered mail before you are charged. But you may receive no registered letter. Instead, you may receive only a visit from the FBI.

Don't ignore a warning letter from the U.S. Attorney or a visit from the FBI. If you get either and don't register, you will probably be prosecuted. Talk with your counselor or a knowledgeable attorney right away.

If the FBI Comes

In the unlikely event that the Justice Department decides to investigate your case, the Federal Bureau of Investigation (FBI) may visit you, your friends, or your family. Anything you or your friends say to an FBI agent can be used against you. It's perfectly legal and usually best to say, politely but firmly, "I do not speak to the FBI."

Do not try to outwit FBI agents. They are trained investigators; you are not. Often information which seems unimportant—e.g., your name and address—can be vital to a draft prosecution. FBI agents often ask questions that seem unrelated to the draft. You don't have to answer their questions, and it's safest not to.

Refusing to talk with the FBI is not a crime. Nor is refusing to let them come into your house (unless they have a search warrant). But if you do speak with them, it's a federal crime to lie to them.

Keep in mind that a visit from the FBI may be the only warning you'll receive that you are going to be prosecuted. If you are visited by the FBI, talk to your counselor or lawyer right away.

Late Registration

Registering after the 60-day period when you are supposed to register does not cure a violation of the law. Even when the government was prosecuting non-registrants in 1980-1981, it did not charge late registrants and usually gave non-registrants several chances to register before it charged them. If you do register late, the government would have to charge you, if at all, within five years after you register. If you never register, you can be charged at any time up to your thirty-first birthday. These are the outside limits. Unless present government policy changes, most likely nothing will happen.

Selective Service will not accept your registration after you reach age 26. This means that if you don't register before your 26th birthday, you might never be able to get a federal student loan or job training. And you might never be able to work for the federal government. See Chapter 16 for details.

Leaving the Country

Throughout U.S. history, many immigrants came to the United States to avoid the draft in their countries. Just the opposite occurred during the Vietnam War: many draft resisters left the U.S. rather than cooperate with the draft. Should draft prosecutions begin again, or should active inductions be resumed, this option might cross your mind as well. By leaving the country, you would avoid immediate prosecution, but this would not solve the problem. Your draft offense wouldn't just go away. If you returned at any point, even for a visit, you could be arrested and prosecuted.

Although President Carter pardoned Vietnam era draft resisters in 1977, you can't count on a pardon or an amnesty if you leave the country. The 1977 Pardon does not apply to future resisters, although amnesties of some sort have been traditional after every U.S. war.

Leaving the country is harder now than during the Vietnam era. Many countries which once took draft resisters have all but closed their borders to immigrants.

What Are the Odds?

No one should violate the law simply because they think they can get away with it. But if you find that your conscience won't let you register with Selective Service, the odds are very good that you will never face federal charges.

A more important question, which is discussed in Chapter 16, is whether you will qualify for student aid and other federal benefits that you may need. Many people who oppose draft registration have felt that they had to compromise on this issue because they couldn't afford to lose federal benefits. If that's your decision, you have plenty of company—and you have nothing to be ashamed of.

Whatever you finally decide to do, it helps if you can talk your decision over with a sympathetic person before you make any commitments. CCCO can help you find a counselor in your community, or if there is none, one of our staff will be glad to talk with you over the telephone.

Chapter 18
Documenting Your CO Claim

You've read this book, thought a lot about the issues, and decided that you're a conscientious objector. What can you do *now* to show that you're a CO?

It's a fair question. Chapter 12 discussed ways of choosing peace in your life. This chapter discusses how to put together evidence that you are a CO. If there's a draft in the future and you're subject to it, you'll need proof that you're sincere. And even if there's no draft, writing about your beliefs and gathering evidence about them can help you to think more clearly about yourself and your values. The first part of this chapter gives ideas on evidence that can support a CO claim. The second part deals with Selective Service's Claim Documentation Form, Conscientious Objector (SSS Form 22). No one knows whether Selective Service will use this form for a future draft, but understanding the questions on it can help you in thinking about your beliefs and preparing yourself just in case.

Your CO File

It's a good idea for you to begin now to keep a "CO file," which could support a future CO claim. Your file needn't be elaborate unless you want it to be. But you may find as you gather material for it that it helps you to think about war and your response to it. Your file should cover four areas:

✔ What you believe and why;

✔ How you came to believe it;

✔ Your sincerity;

✔ Actions that show you believe what you do;

✔ Your file can also include articles, news clippings, and similar material that you've found particularly helpful.

You shouldn't just put documents in your file and never look at them again. Go through it now and then to see if there's anything that's gotten out of date, a supporting letter which you now feel you don't want to use, etc. You'd be surprised how helpful it can be to read, say, something you wrote a few years ago, or to reread a book or article that inspired you earlier in your life.

Showing a History

If you have to apply for CO status under the draft law, you'll increase your chances of being recognized if you can show that your claim isn't a new decision for you. You can use your imagination here. You'll have to because each person is different. Have you ever been on a peace march? Or written letters to the editor, or anti-war poems or short stories? Have you spoken out against war in your school? What about membership in peace groups like the War Resisters League or the Fellowship of Reconciliation?

Some COs keep a kind of "diary" or notebook to keep track of actions that support their claims. Among items that you might include in such a notebook are participation in peace demonstrations, books or articles that you've read, movies, television shows, or plays you've seen, speakers you've heard, and other things which have helped to form your beliefs. You don't have to keep a diary, but it can be helpful in recalling things that happened months or even years ago.

Most churches in this country support conscientious objectors. If your church does, or if it encourages its members to reject war, a statement from your minister (if you have one) and the official position of your church can help to show that you're sincere.

If you're not a member of a church, by the way, joining one of the "peace churches" won't help you to make a CO claim if you ever face the draft. It might even hurt because your local board might think you joined to avoid the draft. You should base your decision about whether to join a church, and which church to join, on what you want to do, not on how it will affect your CO claim.

The CCCO Card

One way to take a stand for your beliefs is to register now with CCCO. CCCO will send you a "CO Registration Card" on request. If you fill the card out and return it, CCCO will keep it on file for you. Then, when you need evidence to support your CO claim, CCCO will send you a statement showing the date you filed. The card itself will remain in CCCO's files for safekeeping.

The CCCO card is *not* an official application for conscientious objector status. It can help to make a stronger claim, but by itself it won't be enough. If you ever face the draft, you'll need to file a formal CO claim with your local board, including the kinds of evidence that this chapter suggests.

Along with CCCO, you can register with your local or national church. The CCCO Card has a space for this which you can fill out and return to your church. Or you can simply write to your church and tell them that you're a conscientious objector. Some churches have a formal national or regional registry. Others don't, but often local churches will accept a registration letter or card.

What Have You Done?

One of the best ways to show your history and sincerity as a CO is to point to actions in your own life. You don't have to be a "political" person to do this. Many COs have never been on a peace march or joined a peace organization—though you may decide you want to do this.

Any action that shows that you live by your beliefs can be helpful. If you've worked for a community center after school or taken a lifesaving course at the Red Cross, make a note of this or a copy of any documents (like a certificate received at the end of lifesaving training) and put it in your CO file. And, of course, note any actions like going on a demonstration.

If you ever make a CO claim under the draft, you will need supporting letters. "Supporting Letters for CO Claims," Appendix II of this book, gives guidelines for these letters.

Writing Your CO Claim

If you have to apply for CO status, you'll need to give a written statement of what you believe. No one knows exactly what questions the Selective Service form will ask if there is a draft in the future. And you may never face the draft. Writing your beliefs down, however, is a good way to clarify and strengthen them.

You don't have to write a book to apply for CO status. The simpler your answers are, the better. If you have trouble writing, you might try talking about your beliefs with a friend or counselor who's taking notes. Or you might try talking about your beliefs to a tape recorder.

Good writing is very much like talking. You don't have to use big words or complicated sentences. If you try to write as you would talk, you'll probably find preparing your claim much easier. Once you have a first draft, you can polish it. The important thing is to get something on paper. When you've done this, you'll probably find that it was easier than you thought.

The Form 22 Questions

The Selective Service questions aren't the only ones that you might write about, but they do cover much what you need to think about as you decide whether you are a CO. Try using them as guidelines.

Question 1 on Form 22 asks: *Describe the beliefs which are the reasons for your claiming conscientious objection to combatant military training and service or to all military training and service.* This question means just what it says. Your problem may be figuring out what it is you believe. Read Chapter 3 of this book to get an idea what kinds of beliefs the law recognizes. You'll note that your religious beliefs are the beliefs—whether you call them religious, moral, ethical, or a mixture—that lead you to be a conscientious objector.

Even though the question reads that way, it's not enough simply to state your beliefs. How do your beliefs lead you to be a conscientious objector? Remember that there are probably thousands, or even millions, of people who have beliefs much like yours but don't object to war. What makes you different? If you have to make a CO claim under the draft, your local board will want to know.

Question 2 asks: *Describe how and when you acquired these beliefs. Your answer may include such information as the influence of family members or other persons; training, if applicable; your personal experiences; membership in organizations; books and readings which influenced you.*

Your CO file, if you have one, will be helpful in answering Question 2. This question gives you a chance to describe your background and, if there's a draft when you are writing your answer, convince your local board that you're sincere. You can include your childhood experiences, early religious training, books you have read, television shows or movies you have seen, people you have talked with, direct or indirect experience with the military—anything that will give a good picture.

If you've ever been in the military (for instance, in Junior ROTC when you were in high school), it's a good idea to tell your local board about this and explain how your views have changed. They can't hold it against you unless you claim that you were a CO at the time you were in the military. Then they'll ask why your beliefs let you join then, but not now. And that would be a good question. Are your beliefs stronger now? Were you really a CO then? Did your time in the military turn you toward being a CO? It does for many people.

A good answer to Question 2 can make for a strong claim. You can organize your answer any way you want, but most COs find it easiest to start in childhood and work up to the present.

What Have You Done?

Questions 3 asks you to: *Explain what most clearly shows that your beliefs are deeply held. You may wish to include a description of how your beliefs affect the way you live.*

For a discussion of "deeply held" beliefs, read Chapter 3. You'll note that "deeply held" beliefs are the same as sincere beliefs. Anything that shows you're sincere will also show that your beliefs are "deeply held." You might try to think of one action or incident that shows your beliefs more strongly than any other, but if you can't, the kind of information suggested for your CO file—such as membership in peace groups—can make a good answer to this question.

Showing how your beliefs influence the way you live isn't always easy. COs are as varied a group of people as any other group—and, just like everyone else, they don't think constantly about war and their lives. You probably don't either. But your concerns about war have probably already made some difference in your life. Think about what that is as you work on your answer to this question. Do you approach people differently because of your beliefs? Does it affect your choice of sports, music, or food—or other choices you make every day? How? Ask yourself these questions and others like them, and you'll have a start on answering Question 3.

One place where your beliefs might make a big difference is in your choice of careers. You'll find some helpful discussion of this issue in Chapter 12. But unless you already have your career planned, you probably won't be able to talk about this in much detail. As a minimum, however, you can make clear what you won't do—for instance, work in a defense plant or join the Army. If you have an idea what career you might want, this is the place to use it. The same goes for spare-time work that you want to do. What's most important is that you show how your values affect what you want to do.

Once You've Written Your Claim

When you've got a first or second draft of your claim, you should take it to a draft counselor and have him or her read it. Your draft counselor can't tell you what to say, but he or she may be able to help you improve the way you say it. And your counselor can spot weaknesses in your claim which you can then rewrite to make a stronger claim.

If you want to test your beliefs, you could show your claim to someone who doesn't agree with you and ask them to criticize your arguments. Getting friendly criticism can help you become more confident in your stand.

Why Write It Down?

Writing can be hard, time-consuming work, and you may have had problems doing it in the past. Why bother when there may never be a draft? Or when you may not even be subject to the draft?

There are many answers to this question. For people

who might face a future draft, one obvious answer is that if inductions begin again and you are called up, you won't have the luxury of time. You may have to decide what to do in less than ten days, and the deadline for your completed CO claim may be almost as strict. Preparing now could save you a lot of trouble in the future.

But writing down your beliefs or talking about them is a good thing to do whether or not you face the draft. Many experienced writers and COs—including the author of this book—find that writing and talking about an issue helps them to think and may lead to important discoveries about themselves. When you talk seriously about an issue, you have to be open to new ideas and arguments, and you have to be willing to support your beliefs with good ideas. Talking things out can clarify a great deal for you.

It's the same with writing. To put your ideas on paper, you have to focus on them, test them, and see whether you can support them with good arguments. At the end of the process you have a much better idea what you think and why. That makes it worth doing if you can—even if you don't end up with a beautifully polished essay. That's not the point. The point is for *you* to discover what *you* believe. Writing and talking seriously about your beliefs can help.

Things to Think About

☞ What have you learned in your life that makes you think you should be a conscientious objector?

☞ What have you done to live by your beliefs—not just your CO beliefs, but *all* your beliefs?

Ideas for Papers

✍ Write out *your* answers to the questions on the Selective Service Claim Form—even if you don't qualify as a conscientious objector.

To Learn More...

A Short Course on War and Peace

A Note from the Author: If you want to learn more about war and peace, you can't depend on any single book, film, or other source of information. In this section, I have chosen 33 books which I think will give you a good understanding of war and conscientious objection. I've included some novels and auto-biographies because they can give a more personal and moving picture of war than a history or a reference book. All the books in this section, however, are well-written and full of information.

You don't, of course, have to read all these books—or even read one book—to be a conscientious objector. But if you want to understand war, these books will help. You can find even more suggestions under "Further Reading."

In each section I've marked one book with a ✔ to show that I think it is the book I think is most important. You don't have to agree with my judgments. I hope you will read all these books and decide for yourself. But the checkmarked books were important for me, and I hope they will be important for you.

A Short Course on War

Barnaby, Frank, ed. *The Gaia Peace Atlas: Survival into the Third Millenium.* New York: Doubleday, 1988.

Thorough and knowledgeable overview of war, peace, the environment, and what it will take to build a secure future. Spectacularly designed book.

Cook, Joan Marble. *In Defense of Homo Sapiens*. New York: Farrar, Straus and Giroux, 1975. PB: New York: Dell—Laurel Edition, 1976.

This easy-to-read book argues that people do not have a "war instinct." The bibliography is excellent for those who want to study the issue further.

✔ Dyer, Gwynne. *War*. New York: Crown Publishers, 1985.

Comprehensive, readable study of war, one of the best yet done. Based on the public television series, this book covers the same material in much greater detail. Though dated by events, it is still an excellent introduction to the subject. Read particularly the chapters on the history of war and the chapter on Marine basic training.

✔ Keegan, John. *A History of Warfare*. New York: Alfred A. Knopf, 1993.

Distinguished historian John Keegan's most important book on military history challenges everyone's ideas about war with many new insights.

Keegan, John, and Richard Holmes. *Soldiers: A History of Men in Battle*. Foreword by Frederick Forsyth. New York: Viking, 1986.

Based on the BBC television series, this is a good general history of warfare as experienced by the troops themselves. Keegan and Holmes do their usual excellent job.

Sivard, Ruth Leger. *World Military and Social Expenditures*. New York: World Policy Institute, 1986. (Available from World Policy Institute, 777 United Nations Plaza, New York, NY 10017, for $5.50 postpaid.).

Definitive short resource on its subject.

Wilson, Andrew. *The Disarmer's Handbook of Military Technology and Organization*. Middlesex, Eng: Penguin, 1983.

Good brief resource on practically all aspects of war, including causes, military command structure, weapons systems, and many other issues. Although much of its discussion of NATO and the Cold War is now dated, it can still help you find your way around in the confusing world of modern warfare.

A Short Course on Peace

✔ Deming, Barbara. *We Are All Part of One Another: A Barbara Deming Reader.* Philadelphia: New Society Publishers, 1984.

Good selection of essays and other writings by a major feminist/pacifist writer.

McSorley, Richard. *The New Testament Basis of Peacemaking.* Washington, D.C.: Center for Peace Studies, Georgetown University, 1979.

A detailed discussion of the New Testament's teachings on war.

Seeley, Robert, and Aldous Huxley. *A Handbook of Non-Violence, including Aldous Huxley's Encyclopedia of Pacifism.* Westport, Ct.: Lawrence Hill & Co./ Lakeville Press, 1986.

Wide-ranging collection of articles on war, peace, and nonviolence. Huxley's *Encyclopedia* is considered a pacifist classic.

Tollefson, James W. *The Strength Not to Fight: An Oral History of Conscientious Objectors of the Vietnam War.* Boston: Little, Brown, 1993.

Detailed stories of Vietnam-era COs, arranged by topics to form an overall history of what it was like to be a CO during that period.

Vanderhaar, Gerard A. *Christians and Nonviolence in the Nuclear Age.* Mystic, Ct.: Twenty-Third Publications, 1982.

Good brief introduction to Christian pacifism and nonviolence from a Catholic theologian and professor of religion.

Walzer, Michael. *Just and Unjust Wars.* New York: Basic Books, 1977.

Interesting modern update of the Just War theory. Worth reading even if you don't agree with it—or perhaps especially when you don't agree with it.

Alternatives to Violence

Anzalone, Joan, ed. *Good Works: A Guide to Careers in Social Change.* New York: W. W. Norton, 1985.

Readable and useful book on practical alternatives to non-change-oriented work.

Ash, Timothy Garton. *The Polish Revolution: Solidarity.* New York: Charles Scribner's Sons, 1983.

Detailed history and reflections on Solidarity, the Polish government's response, the Western response, and its significance.

Bondurant, Joan. *The Conquest of Violence.* Berkeley, CA: University of California Press, 1965. PB available.

A study of the philosophy and strategy of Gandhian nonviolent direct action.

✔ Cooney, Robert, and Helen Michalowski. *The Power of the People: Active Nonviolence in the United States.* Philadelphia: New Society Publishers, 1986.

Well-done picture history of the nonviolent movements in the United States.

Hallie, Philip. *Lest Innocent Blood Be Shed: The Story of the Village of Le Chambon and How Goodness Happened There.* New York: Harper & Row, 1979. PB available.

The amazing history of how one French village organized, quietly and nonviolently, to save the lives of thousands of Jews during World War II.

Judson, Stephanie, ed. *A Manual on Nonviolence and Children.* Philadelphia: New Society Publishers, 1984.

One of the basic texts for people who want to teach peace to children.

Jurgensmeyer, Mark. *Fighting With Gandhi: A Step-by-Step Strategy for Resolving Everyday Conflicts.* San Francisco: Harper & Row, 1984.

Clearly and simply written explanation of basic principles and practice of Gandhian nonviolence.

King, Martin Luther, Jr. *Strength to Love.* Philadelphia: Fortress Press, 1981.

A collection of King's essays detailing his belief in nonviolence.

Zinn, Howard. *A People's History of the United States.* New York: Harper Colophon Books, 1980.

Well-written history tells the story of the U.S. from the viewpoint of ordinary people and those in the various movements for social change.

The Peace Movement

Peace, Roger C., III. *A Just and Lasting Peace: The U.S. Peace Movement from the Cold War to Desert Storm.* Chicago, Il.: The Noble Press, 1991.

Comprehensive book on recent developments in the peace movement.

✔ Schlissel, Lillian, ed. *Conscience in America.* New York: Dutton, 1968. PB available.

A documentary history of conscientious objection in America, this is a good collection of historic documents, both well- and little-known.

Wittner, Lawrence S. *Rebels Against War—American Peace Movement 1941-1983.* Philadelphia: Temple University Press, 1984.

Histories of major peace organizations in the United States. Emphasis on SANE, War Resisters League, and Fellowship of Reconciliation.

Novels and Personal Stories

Ehrhart, W. D. *Vietnam-Perkasie: A Combat Marine Memoir.* Jefferson, N.C.: MacFarland & Co., 1983.

Excellent semi-fictional, semi-autobiographical book on one Marine's experiences during the Vietnam War.

Everett, Melissa. *Breaking Ranks.* Philadelphia: New Society Publishers, 1989.

Stories of ten men who left jobs in the military, the intelligence community, or the Pentagon for reasons of conscience.

Hemingway, Ernest. *A Farewell to Arms.* New York: Scribner's, 1929.

One of the great war novels, this tells the story of an ambulance driver on the Italian front in World War I and the woman he loved.

✔ Herr, Michael. *Dispatches.* New York: Alfred A. Knopf, 1977.

Herr presents the Vietnam War in a powerful way through his own experiences and those of others in Vietnam.

Remarque, Erich Maria. *All Quiet on the Western Front,* trans. by A. W. Wheen. Boston: Little, Brown, 1929. PB: Greenwich, CT: Fawcett, 1978.

This classic novel shows World War I from a German enlisted soldier's point of view.

Van Devanter, Lynda, with Christopher Morgan. *Home Before Morning.* New York/Toronto: Beaufort Books, 1983.

An autobiography of an Army nurse in Vietnam, this book reveals a side of the war which is not well known.

Vonnegut, Kurt, Jr. *Slaughterhouse-Five.* New York: Delacorte Press, 1969. PB available.

Vonnegut's only war novel tells the story of Billy Pilgrim, who was a prisoner of war caught in the firebombing of Dresden.

Further Reading

War in Literature

Novels

Crane, Stephen. *The Red Badge of Courage*, restoration and introduction by Henry Binder. New York: Avon Books, 1982.

The only popularly available edition of this Civil War novel as the author originally wrote it.

Del Vecchio, John. *The 13th Valley*. New York: Bantam, 1982

This semi-autobiographical account of an infantry unit in Vietnam recreates the day-by-day horror of Vietnam.

Heller, Joseph. *Catch-22*. New York: Simon & Schuster, 1961. PB available.

Set in World War II, this is the best modern satire on war and the military.

Tolstoy, Leo. *War and Peace*. Available in many editions and translations

Considered by some the greatest novel ever written, this is an account of Napoleon's invasion of Russia and much, much more.

Trumbo, Dalton. *Johnny Got His Gun*. New York: Bantam Books, 1978. PB

This powerful novel tells of a war veteran who was wounded in combat and has lost his arms, legs, eyes, and ability to speak.

One of the most famous anti-war books.

Poetry

Bates, Scott. *Poems of War Resistance*. New York: Grossman Publishers, 1969. OP

A beautiful collection of poems from 2300 B.C. to the present.

Parsons, I.M., ed. *Men Who March Away: Poems of the First World War*. New York: The Viking Press, 1965..

A good selection of poems by the men in the trenches (Wilfred Owen, Siegfried Sassoon, etc.) and civilians who saw the war from England.

Autobiography

Arnett, Peter. *Live from the Battlefield: From Vietnam to Baghdad: 35 Years in the World's War Zones*. New York: Simon & Schuster, 1993

Excellent autobiography by one of the most distinguished war correspondents of the post-World War II era.

Brittain, Vera. *Testament of Youth*. New York: Wideview Books, 1980.

Powerful autobiography by a major British anti-war activist. Shows World War I as seen by a nurse who worked at the front lines.

Caputo, Philip. *A Rumor of War*. New York: Holt, Rinehart & Winston, 1977.

Probably the best-known combat memoir to come out of the Indochina War, in which Caputo was an infantry officer.

cummings, e.e. *The Enormous Room*. New York: Liveright, 1970. PB available.

An account of the prison experiences of the poet who, with a friend, was arrested by the French government while serving as an ambulance driver during World War I.

Kovic, Ron. *Born on the Fourth of July.* New York: McGraw-Hill, 1976. PB: Pocket Books, 1978.

Autobiography of a wounded and paralyzed Vietnam veteran who joined the anti-war movement. Kovic spares the reader none of his pain.

Mowat, Farley. *And No Birds Sang.* Boston: Atlantic Monthly Press, 1979.

A powerful story of what it was like to be a Canadian infantryman during World War II.

War in History

Diplomatic History

Herken, Gregg. *The Winning Weapon: The Atomic Bomb in the Cold War, 1945-1950.* New York: Alfred A. Knopf, 1980.

Well-documented history traces the U.S. attempt to establish and maintain nuclear superiority in the years just after World War II.

Knightly, Philip. *The First Casualty: From the Crimea to Vietnam: The War Correspondent as Hero, Propagandist, and Myth Maker.* New York and London: Harcourt, Brace, Jovanovich, 1975. PB available.

This lively book tells how, since about 1850, newspaper and broadcast reporters have covered wars.

Lafore, Laurence. *The End of Glory: An Interpretation of the Origins of World War II.* Philadelphia and New York: J.B. Lippincott, 1970. PB available.

A careful treatment of the roots of the Second World War, this book traces the war's origins to the breakdown of the old order in Europe beginning before World War I.

Taylor, A. J. P. *The Origins of the Second World War.* New York: Atheneum, 1961 (OP). PB: Greenwich, Ct.: Fawcett, 1961.

A well-known historian argues that the Allies deserve some of the blame for World War II.

Pre-World War I History

Horne, Alistair. *The Fall of Paris: The Siege and the Commune 1870-71*. New York: St. Martin's Press, 1965.

Well-written and very thorough history of the 1870 war between Prussia and France, the Siege of Paris, and the Paris Commune.

Pakenham, Thomas. *The Boer War*. New York: Random House, 1979.

The most exhaustive general history of the Boer War, arguably the first guerrilla war of the 20th Century.

Ward, Geoffrey C., Ric Burns, and Ken Burns. *The Civil War: An Illustrated History*. New York: Alfred A. Knopf, 1991.

Richly detailed companion book to the excellent Public Television series on the Civil War.

World War I

Macdonald, Lyn. *Somme*. London: Michael Joseph, 1983.

Vivid and ultimately moving reconstruction, much of it in the words of survivors, of one of the bloodiest battles of World War I.

Moorehead, Alan. *Gallipoli*. New York: Harper & Row, 1956.

Excellent history of the 1915 British operation against Turkey, one of the great military disasters of World War I.

Moorhouse, Geoffrey. *Hell's Foundations: A Town, Its Myths & Gallipoli*. London: Sceptre Press, 1992.

Powerful study of the effects of a World War I battle on a small English cities that supplied the troops for one regiment.

Tuchman, Barbara. *The Guns of August*. New York: MacMillan, 1962.

Vivid, detailed history of the beginning of World War I and the Battle of the Marne.

Wolff, Leon. *In Flanders Fields: The 1917 Campaign.* New York: The Viking Press, 1958.

Well-written history of the Third Battle of Ypres. Wolff skillfully interweaves political developments and events on the battlefield.

World War II

Keegan, John. *The Second World War.* New York: Viking, 1989.

Keegan's complete history of World War II divides its coverage into narrative, strategic analysis, battle pieces, and "theme of war." Excellent introduction on the background of the war, with perceptive essay on the war's aftermath at the end of the book.

McKee, Alexander. *Dresden 1945: The Devil's Tinderbox.* New York: E. P. Dutton, 1984.

Impassioned history of the Dresden bombing, with material on the Allied bombing campaign and its ideology, by a former member of the British Army who saw the destruction caused by bombing in many European cities.

Salisbury, Harrison. *The 900 Days: The Siege of Leningrad.* New York: Harper & Row, 1969.

Horrifying and detailed account of the greatest siege of modern times.

Terkel, Studs. *"The Good War": An Oral History of World War Two.* New York: Pantheon Books, 1984.

Well-done, comprehensive oral history of World War II.

Postwar Era

Goulden, Joseph C. *Korea: The Untold Story of the War.* New York: Times Books, 1980.

Detailed history of the Korean War based on material released to the author under the Freedom of Information Act.

The Nature of War

Combat

Keegan, John. *The Face of Battle: A Study of Agincourt, Waterloo, and the Somme.* New York: Viking Press, 1976. PB: New York, Vintage Books, 1977.

This fascinating book tries to reconstruct battles as seen by the soldiers who fought.

Women in the Military

Enloe, Cynthia. *Does Khaki Become You? The Militarization of Women's Lives.* Boston: South End Press, 1983. PB

A full treatment of the issues raised by the increasing use of women by the military.

Saywell, Shelley. *Women in War: First-Hand Accounts from World War II to El Salvador.* New York: Viking, 1985.

Fascinating collection of recollections by women who experienced war as soldiers, many of them as direct combatants.

Blacks in the Military

Mullen, R. W. *Blacks in America's Wars.* New York: Monad Press, 1973. PB: Pathfinder Press, 1974.

Covers the experiences of black troops in wars from the Revolution to Vietnam.

Terry, Wallace. *Bloods: An Oral History of the Vietnam War by Black Veterans.* New York: Random House, 1984.

A series of interviews with black troops, ranging from enlisted people and draftees to career officers.

Gays in the Military

Bourdonnay, Katherine, et al, ed. *Fighting Back: Lesbian and Gay Draft, Military and Veterans Issues.* Chicago: National Lawyers Guild Military Law Task Force, 1985.

Definitive resource on its subject.

Causes of War

Lorenz, Konrad. *On Aggression.* New York: Harcourt, Brace & World, 1966. PB: Harcourt, Brace, Jovanovich, 1974.

Lorenz, who is famous for his animal studies, here traces the roots of war to a human "killer instinct."

Modern Warfare

Nuclear War

Ehrlich, Paul, Carl Sagan, and others. *The Cold and the Dark: Life After Nuclear War.* New York: W. W. Norton, 1984.

The first complete discussion of the "nuclear winter," based on papers delivered at the conference which announced the findings of a research group headed by Carl Sagan.

Freeman, Harold. *If You Give a Damn About Life.* New York: Dodd, Mead, 1985.

Clear and basic discussion of nuclear weapons and their effects, arms control, etc.

Hersey, John. *Hiroshima.* New York: Alfred A. Knopf, 1969. PB available.

A powerful report on six survivors of the Hiroshima bombing and what they went through when the bomb hit.

Guerrilla Warfare

Laqueur, Walter. *Guerrilla: A Historical and Critical Study*. Boston: Little, Brown, 1976.

One of the most detailed works available on guerrilla warfare. Includes a chronology of guerrilla warfare in the last hundred years. The number of wars on the list will surprise many readers.

Terrorism

Meltzer, Milton. *The Terrorists*. New York: Harper & Row, 1983.

Clear and concise introduction to the history of political terrorism from the 11th Century to the present. Includes a well-balanced chapter on state-sponsored terror.

Former Yugoslavia

Dizdarevic, Zlatko. *Sarajevo: A War Journal*, trans by Anselm Hollo; ed. by Ammiel Alcalay. New York: Fromm International, 1993.

Moving personal account of life in Sarajevo during the Bosnian Civil War.

Genocide

The Holocaust

Davidowicz, Lucy. *The War Against the Jews, 1933-1945*. New York: Holt, Rinehart & Winston, 1975.

A recent, well-researched, and detailed history of the Holocaust.

Wyman, David S. *The Abandonment of the Jews: America and the Holocaust 1941-1945*. New York: Pantheon Books, 1984.

Details how the U.S. and other Allies did little to save European Jews threatened with extermination. Also discusses what could have been done and rescue proposals made at the time.

Nazism

Bullock, Alan. *Hitler, A Study in Tyranny*. New York: Harper Colophon Books, 1964.

Massive study of Hitler, still one of the best available.

Current Political Issues

Military Industrial Complex

Adams, Gordon. *The Iron Triangle: The Politics of Defense Contracting*. New Brunswick, N.J.: Transaction Books, 1981.

Detailed discussion of the interlocking relationships between U.S. defense contractors and the U.S. military.

Central America

Clements, Charles, M.D. *Witness to War: An American Doctor in El Salvador*. New York: Bantam Books, 1984.

Moving story of how an Air Force pilot who flew missions in Vietnam changed his mind, became a doctor, and went to El Salvador to care for people regardless of which side they were on in the guerrilla war. One of the few accounts of life in rebel-held territory.

Middle East

American Friends Service Committee. *A Compassionate Peace: A Future for the Middle East*. New York: Hill and Wang, 1982.

Balanced effort to find a way out of the impasse in the Middle East. Somewhat dated but still useful.

Russia and the Former Soviet Union

Shipler, David. K. *Russia: Broken Idols, Solemn Dreams.* New York: Times Books, 1983. PB: New York: Viking Penguin, 1984.

Thoughtful and readable journalistic memoir and study of the Soviet system and the people of the Soviet Union. Contains many anecdotes and interviews and some first-rate Russian jokes which are even more revealing than the interviews.

Smith, Hedrick. *The New Russians.* New York: Random House, 1990.

Update and expansion of Smith's previous book on the Soviet Union takes into account developments since the advent of Mikhail Gorbachev. Written and published before the breakup of the Soviet Union.

The Indochina War

Vietnam History

Karnow, Stanley. *Vietnam: A History.* New York: Viking, 1983.

A companion to the public television series, this is the first complete popular history of the Vietnam War.

Maclear, Michael. *The Ten Thousand Day War: Vietnam: 1945-1975.* New York: Avon Books, 1981.

Readable and detailed military and political history of the U.S. involvement in Vietnam.

MacPherson, Myra. *Long Time Passing: Vietnam and the Haunted Generation.* Garden City, N.Y.: Doubleday, 1984.

Well-done history of the Vietnam era as seen by many different people—soldiers, anti-war activists, etc.—who lived through it.

Vietnam Peace Movement

Zaroulis, Nancy, and Gerald Sullivan. *Who Spoke Up? American Protest Against the War in Vietnam, 1963-1975*. Garden City, N.Y.: Doubleday & Co., 1984.

A detailed study, not only of the peace movement, but of the government's reaction to it and of public attitudes toward the war. Portrays the public movement and its private agonies, and does its job well. Essential reading for all Americans.

Vietnam Personal Stories

Bryan, C. D. B. *Friendly Fire*. New York: Putnam, 1976.

True story of a family's search for the truth about the death of their son, who was killed in Vietnam by U.S. fire.

Vietnam Analysis

Taylor, Telford. *Nuremberg and Vietnam: An American Tragedy*. New York: Times Books, 1970.

A critique of the Vietnam War on grounds of international law and the Nuremberg principles, by one of the Nuremberg prosecutors.

Building Peace

Arms Control and Disarmament

Foell, Earl, and Richard Henneman, eds. *How Peace Came to the World*. Cambridge, Mass.: MIT Press, 1986.

Varied collection of essays selected from those submitted to the Christian Science Monitor's "Peace 2010" contest.

Joseph, Paul, and Simon Rosenblum, eds. *Search for Sanity: Nuclear Weapons and Disarmament*. Boston: South End Press, 1984.

Wide-ranging collection of articles on every aspect of nuclear weapons and war. An excellent resource.

Walker, Paul. *Seizing the Initiative: First Steps to Disarmament.* Philadelphia and Nyack, N.Y.: American Friends Service Committee and Fellowship of Reconciliation, 1983.

A study of arms control agreements. Concludes that such agreements have always had significant gaps that allowed the arms race to continue, and recommends instead unilateral initiatives for disarmament.

Pacifism

Lynd, Alice, ed. *We Won't Go.* Boston: Beacon Press, 1968.

An excellent collection of statements by Vietnam-era war resisters, with many different positions and viewpoints.

Mayer, Peter, ed. *The Pacifist Conscience.* New York: Holt, Rinehart & Winston, 1966. OP

Alternatives to violence from early times to the present. Contains an excellent reading list.

McSorley, Richard. *The New Testament Basis of Peacemaking.* Washington, D.C.: Center for Peace Studies, Georgetown University, 1979.

A detailed discussion of the New Testament's teachings on war.

Thoreau, Henry David. "On the Duty of Civil Disobedience." In *Walden and Other Writings.* Garden City, N.Y.:: Doubleday, 1970. (Many other editions.)

One of the basic texts on civil disobedience and resistance to unjust laws. Influenced Gandhi, draft resistance, etc.

Yoder, John H. *What Would You Do?.* Scottdale, Pa.: Herald Press, 1983.

Interesting discussion of various moral questions on the use of force which confront pacifists and everyone else.

History of Pacifism

Bainton, Roland H. *Christian Attitudes Toward War and Peace: A Historical Survey and Critical Re-Evaluation.* New York: Abingdon Press, 1960. PB available.

The author examines the writings of the church fathers and evolving Christian attitudes toward participation in war, showing how Christians came to terms with the state

Meltzer, Milton. *Ain't Gonna Study War No More: The Story of America's Peace Seekers.* New York: Harper & Row, 1985.

Easy-to-read biographies of peacemakers such as Thoreau, Jane Addams, etc.

Conscientious Objection

Axelrad, Albert S. *Call to Conscience: Jews, Judaism, and Conscientious Objection.* Hoboken, NJ: Ktav Publishing House, 1986

Thorough and informed discussion of the theological and philosophical basis of Jewish conscientious objection, draft procedures, etc

National Interreligious Service Board for Conscientious Objectors. *Words of Conscience: Religious Statements on Conscientious Objection.* Washington, D.C.: NISBCO, 1983.

The best collection of official church statements—including Native American, Nation of Islam, etc.—on conscientious objection.

War Resistance

Kohn, Stephen M. *Jailed for Peace: The History of American Draft Law Violators, 1658-1985.* Connecticut: Greenwood Press, 1986

Concise history of American draft resistance

Zahn, Gordon C. *In Solitary Witness: The Life and Death of Franz Jagerstatter*. Collegeville, Mn.: The Liturgical Press, 1981. OP

Biography and reflections on Jagerstatter, an Austrian peasant who refused induction into the Nazi army and was beheaded in 1943.

Personal Stories

Gioglio, Gerald R. *Days of Decision: An Oral History of Conscientious Objectors in the Military During the Vietnam War*. Trenton, NJ: Broken Rifle Press, 1989.

Powerful and moving group of stories from men who took the CO position in the military during the Vietnam era. Includes men who sought discharge, noncombatants, and resisters who ended up in military prisons.

Non-Violence

Nonviolence Theory

Bondurant, Joan. *The Conquest of Violence*. Berkeley, Ca: University of California Press, 1965. PB available.

A study of the philosophy and strategy of Gandhian non-violent direct action.

Gandhi, Mohandas K. *The Essential Gandhi: His Life, Work and Ideas, edited by Louis Fischer*. New York: Random House/Vintage Books, 1962.

Wide-ranging selection from Gandhi's writings arranged in biographical order.

Gregg, Richard. *The Power of Non-Violence*. New York: Schocken, 1959. 2nd Ed.: Nyack, N.Y.: Fellowship, 1959. PB: Schocken, 1959.

The classic treatment of Gandhi's nonviolent philosophy and its relation to nonviolence in the West.

King, Martin Luther, Jr. *The Trumpet of Conscience*. New York:

Harper & Row, 1968.

King's last book covers nonviolence and social change, Vietnam, and other topics. A beautiful Christmas sermon on peace ends the book.

Lakey, George. *Strategy for a Living Revolution.* New York: Grossman Publishers, 1973.

A major work on nonviolent methods for gaining social justice.

Lynd, Staughton, ed. *Non-Violence in America: A Documentary History.* Indianapolis, Ind.: Bobbs-Merrill, 1966. PB available.

A good collection of essays on American nonviolence.

Sharp, Gene. *The Politics of Non-Violent Action.* Boston: Porter Sargent, 1973. PB available.

Sharp's major work on nonviolence, this book is a basic resource for everyone interested in alternatives to war.

Tolstoy, Leo. *The Kingdom of God Is Within You,* trans. by Leo Weiner. New York: Farrar, Straus and Cudahy, 1961. PB

An interpretation of the Sermon on the Mount, this is the major statement of Tolstoy's belief in nonviolence.

History of Nonviolence

Sibley, Mulford Q. *The Quiet Battle.* Boston: Beacon Press, 1969. OP

A good selection of essays on nonviolence, ranging from the Bible to Martin Luther King, Jr., and Albert Luthuli. Good introduction.

Practice of Nonviolence

Hedemann, Ed., ed. *War Resisters League Organizer's Manual.* New York: War Resisters League, 1981.

A practical guide to peace action, including organizing demonstrations, printing literature, etc.

Films

Many feature films on war present alternatives to the usual viewpoints. A sampling of these films appears below.

All Quiet on the Western Front (starring Lew Ayres)

This film, which won an Oscar, includes some humorous discussion of the causes of war and the follies of rulers. The ending is one of the most famous in film history.

A Bridge Too Far (all-star case including Liv Ullman, Lord Olivier, Anthony Hopkins, Robert Redford, and Sean Connery)

Intended by producer Joseph E. Levine as an anti-war statement, this film portrays the Allied operation at Arnhem, Holland, in 1944. Excellent battle footage leads to a moving ending showing the plight of war's victims.

Coming Home (starring Jane Fonda and Jon Voight)

This portrayal of the relationship between a wounded Vietnam veteran and a soldier's wife makes a strong statement about Vietnam and all wars.

The King of Hearts (starring Alan Bates and Genevieve Bujold; directed by Phillippe deBroca)

A fine World War I satire that raises the question whether "sane" people who fight in wars are really sane at all.

Some Groups That Work for Peace and Justice

American Friends Service Committee, 1501 Cherry St., Philadelphia, PA 19102

Amnesty International, 2112 Broadway, New York, NY 10023

Center for War/Peace Studies, 218 E. 18th St., New York, NY 10003

Fellowship of Reconciliation, Box 271, Nyack, NY 10960

Friends Committee on National Legislation, 245 2nd St., NE, Washington, DC 20002

National Interreligious Service Board for Conscientious Objectors, Suite 1400, 1612 K Street NW, Washington, DC 20006

Southern Christian Leadership Conference, 334 Auburn Ave., NE, Atlanta, GA 30303

War Resisters League, 339 Lafayette St., New York, NY 10012

Women's International League for Peace and Freedom, 1213 Race St., Philadelphia, PA 19107

Appendices

Appendix 1
Supporting Letters for CO Claims

An important part of your CO claim will be letters to show that you are sincere. You can get supporting letters from friends, family, teachers, ministers, or other people who know you and have some standing in the community. These people don't have to agree with your position. They do have to believe, and say, that you're sincere. It's probably not a good idea to gather letters too much in advance because old letters won't be as effective as recent ones. But you can think about who you might ask to support you, and, if you like, talk with these people to explain what you want them to do if needed.

It's likely that your references won't know how to write a letter for a CO. Here are some guidelines that should help:

✔ A good supporting letter is first a character reference. Your reference doesn't have to know all the details of your claim. He or she does have to know is that you're an honest person who means what you say.

✔ Supporting letters should tell how your reference knows you, how long he or she has known you, and how closely.

✔ The letter should be as brief as possible. One page of single-spaced typing is a good length to try for.

✔ Typed letters and letters on letterhead are very impressive. But a neatly handwritten letter is okay, too. It's important for your claim to be as easy as possible to read.

If you decide to ask people to write supporting letters now, keep the letters in your CO file, and look over them from time to time to make sure you still want to use them as part of your CO claim. If for some reason they seem out of date, you may want to ask for new letters.

Appendix 2
A Health Care Draft?

Health care workers, such as doctors, dentists, and nurses, face special problems in thinking about the military. If you're considering a career in health care, you need to know about the proposed "Health Care Professionals Delivery System," a special draft for health care workers developed by the Selective Service System in the early 1990s.

In August, 1993, Selective Service sought public comments on a "concept paper" on the health care draft. This paper describes the health care draft as Selective Service now conceives of it.

Status of the Proposal

The Selective Service proposal is not in force. It would require authorizing legislation from Congress and implementing regulations. According to Selective Service, it will be kept in reserve to be implemented when needed.

The proposed health care draft would cover sixty-two categories of health care workers, ranging from orthopedic surgeons to animal care technicians. Women would be included in the proposed draft. The proposed draft would cover both men and women up to age 55. (Both of these provisions would require amendments to the Selective Service law.) Health care students would not be covered, but would be required to register when they had qualified for their professions.

How Likely Is It?

Although a return to conscription under the old Selective Service System is unlikely (see Chapter 14 of this book), a health care workers draft would be a possibility in the event of a long war, even one that did not require full mobilization as described in Appendix 1. The military is chronically short of medical specialists, and modern warfare can lead to very heavy casualties and demand for medical services.

If there is a major war or a long but low-level U.S. military involvement, as discussed in Chapter 14, a draft for medical specialists could be set up *before* the government returned to conscription for regular soldiers.

Deferments, Exemptions, and Conscientious Objection

The deferments and exemptions which would be available under a regular draft would also be available to medical specialists. The physical standards for medical specialists are lower than those for regular soldiers, so failing one's physical examination would be more difficult.

Conscientious objectors would be able to apply for and receive assignment to alternative service under the same criteria as those used in the regular draft. Because of the problems the military has in recruiting medical specialists, draft officials might be less likely to grant CO status to a medical specialist CO.

What Should I Do Now?

As noted above, the Selective Service health care draft proposal is just that—a proposal which is not yet embodied in either legislation or new draft regulations. It may never be implemented. In the meantime, be sure to follow the suggestions in Chapter 2 to protect yourself against a possible health care draft. You may find it helpful to write down your beliefs as discussed in Chapter 18. And you should keep in touch with CCCO or one of the national agencies listed under "Some Groups That Work for Peace."

Above all, don't panic. There is no health care workers draft now. The government could not implement such a draft without legislation and public debate. If you've thought about what you believe and followed the suggestions in this book, you should be well-prepared for whatever happens.

Appendix 3
The Mobilization Draft

According to plans in effect as of 1991, only at the last moment, after the declaration of a national defense emergency or a declaration of war, would inductions be resumed. The total force policy developed by the Department of Defense in the mid-seventies requires the use of reserve troops before the use of draftees. Under this policy there are five separate levels of mobilization of reserves, in the following order:

✔ Selected mobilization for domestic contingencies; and for military contingencies:

✔ Presidential 200,000 callup;

✔ Partial mobilization (up to 500,000);

✔ Full mobilization (1,000,000); and

✔ Total mobilization, which includes the use of the draft.

The President would have the power to induct only after an amendment is passed by Congress changing the date of the expiration of the induction authority in the Military Selective Service Act. The Act itself remains in place, but as this book went to press only parts of it, such as registration, were active.

The Draft Lottery

After a declaration of full mobilization, perhaps on the very night of the declaration, a lottery would be held to match, at random, numbers from 1 to 366 to the dates in the calendar year, which are the dates of registrants' birthdays. Registrants would be assigned these random sequence numbers (RSNs) according to their matching birthdates. For example, if you were born on May 15 and May 15 received #12 in the lottery, your RSN would be #12.

Registrants would be divided into a series of "selection groups" based on the year of their birth. The "prime selection group" (the group that will be drafted first) would be made up of those whose 20th birthdays occurred in the current calendar year. The next lower selection group (the "Age 21 Selection Group") would be made up of registrants whose 20th birthdays occurred in the *previous* calendar year, and so on. In each selection group, Selective Service would start with the lowest RSN and go all the way to 366 before it would start calling registrants from older selection groups.

The morning after the lottery, orders to report for induction (for persons classified 1-A, eligible for callup) would be sent by Mailgram to those who have low numbers and are in the "prime selection group." The first groups of draftees would be required to appear in 10 to 13 days to be inducted into the Army. These induction stations are called Military Entrance and Processing Stations (MEPS).

If you are in the prime selection group, no matter how high your number, you might be included in the induction orders issued in the emergency. You should immediately prepare to make your CO claim. In a major war, as many as 650,000 inductees might be called in the first six months. Fewer than 2,000,000 men turn 18 in any calendar year. Selective Service must assume that half of them will not qualify because they are physically or mentally unfit (4-F) and that still others will have postponements, deferments, and exemptions. This will increase the chances that you will be called up.

Applying for Reclassification

The induction orders will instruct draftees about what to do to initiate a claim for any deferment or exemption. Since all inductees will have been automatically classified 1-A (Available for Military Service), you must apply to be reclassified.

The Mailgram will tell you that you may go to the Post Office or a Selective Service Area Office to get a copy of Selective Service's leaflet, "Information for Registrants." It will also tell you that you can obtain and complete a claim form (SSS Form 9, Postponement and Reclassification) and send it to your Selective Service Area Office.

"Information for Registrants" gives a brief overview of the classifications for which you might qualify. It does not give complete information about them, about your rights, or about time limits. Copies of this booklet are available from CCCO. You might want to get one now to have the Selective Service explanation of your options.

File Form 9 with the Area Office of Selective Service which is given on your Mailgram. If you can't get Form 9, send a letter requesting reclassification and specifically stating that you are a conscientious objector to war in any form by reason of your religious or moral beliefs. Section 8 of Form 9 allows you to request a postponement of induction until the end of the semester if you are attending school full-time. In Section 9 there is a check-box to make your claim for 1-0 (CO available for civilian alternative service) or 1-A-0 (CO available for noncombatant military duty) status. If you think you qualify for any other classifications, you should apply for them also. If you do not, you will have waived your right to be considered for them.

Be sure to sign and date your claim. You must get Form 9 postmarked or to the Area Office by the day before you are to appear to be examined. If you don't and your pass your Army physical, you will be inducted or have to refuse induction. You will have lost the opportunity to make your claim.

If because of circumstances beyond your control you can't meet the filing deadline, you can submit your claim at MEPS. This is risky, however, and you should consult your draft counselor or attorney as to how to proceed.

Selective Service will send you SSS Form 22 (Claim Documentation Form—Conscientious Objector) immediately after they receive your Form 9. You will probably have ten days to return the completed Form 22 with supporting documents. Selective Service will also schedule you for a physical examination at MEPS in seven days, and for a personal appearance before your local "claims board" within ten days or more.

Selective Service will order you to report to MEPS so that, if you fail the Army physical, they can classify you 4-F and will not have to complete processing on your CO claim. If you have conscientious reservations about attending the examination, you can obtain a waiver of the examination from the Selective

Service Area Office. Selective Service will then process your CO claim without the Army examination.

Applying for CO Status

For a discussion of Selective Service Form 22 and the questions on it, see Chapter 6. You will find more information about supporting letters in Appendix 2 of this book.

Your answers to the questions on Form 22 should be on sheets of paper that you attach to the form. Be sure to date and sign them. You will want to make several copies so that you, your witnesses, and your draft counselor have a chance to go over your answers. If there's time, you should go over your answers with your counselor *before* you submit them.

Other Classifications

If you meet certain legal standards, you may receive a deferment or exemption which will "supersede" your induction order. This means you won't be drafted as long as you qualify for deferment or exemption. The most common current options are:

✔ *Deferred because of hardship to dependents:* If your family would suffer financially, emotionally, or physically because you were away on military duty, you may qualify for hardship deferment.

✔ *Physically, mentally, or morally unacceptable for military duty:* If you have a medical or psychiatric record or a police record, you may fail the military physical examination. You will need a doctor's letter to prove your case.

✔ *Homosexuality:* Military regulations allow for discharge of gay people who make their sexual preferences public while in the military. Gay people who wish to enlist may do so, provided that they do not make their sexual preference public. The military does not seek information on sexual preference at the time of enlistment or induction. If you're gay, you'll have to decide for yourself whether you want to make this known to military officials at MEPS. If you're not gay, telling military officials that you are is against federal law. It's not an easy decision to make. Before you decide what to do, talk to your counselor. CCCO can also send you more information.

✔ *Minister or divinity student:* If you are a minister who

regularly teaches and preaches your faith, or a full time student preparing for the ministry, you may qualify for deferment or exemption.

✔ *Surviving son:* If your father, mother, or one or more of your sisters or brothers was killed as a result of military duty or is a prisoner of war or missing in action, you may qualify for exemption.

✔ Active duty military personnel and certain public officials are exempt from induction.

Your Personal Appearance

If you're applying for conscientious objector status, your local board will automatically schedule you for a personal appearance. If you don't go to your personal appearance, you will be given another chance to appear. If you again don't appear, the local board will "deem" your claim to be withdrawn. Your local board can excuse a failure to appear if you provide a good reason—e.g., that you were ill—within five days after you failed to appear.

Your personal appearance is your chance to present your claim and show that you're sincere. You'll probably be asked some difficult questions. It's not important to have answers to those questions. In fact, it's often better not to. Answer as best you can, and, if you find a question hard, say so. The important thing is to make clear that you object to war. Often a sincere statement that you haven't worked out all your ideas gives a better impression than a glib answer.

You might want to get some of your friends to fire questions at you, much the way your local board will do. This will give you practice in expressing your beliefs and, if your friends are good actors, dealing with your local board's hostility.

When you appear before your local board, you have the right to present three witnesses. It's also a good idea to take an advisor with you, as is your right. Your advisor can be your attorney or your draft counselor. He or she should be someone who knows the draft law and is familiar with your claim. If your local board asks you a tricky question, you have the right to confer with your advisor. Your advisor, however, can't speak for you.

If you don't speak English well, you should ask for an

interpreter. You are allowed to have one. And, though an attorney can't speak for you before your local board, you can have an attorney appear as a witness.

Recording devices and verbatim transcripts (like that made by a court reporter) are not permitted at personal appearances. You can, however, write down from *memory* a summary of what was said at your personal appearance. And you should. Your local board will file its own summary, and you should give your point of view on what happened. The summary should be in dialogue form if you can remember that well. Your witnesses can help you to remember and corroborate your account. When you've completed your summary, make a copy of it for your own records, get it notarized if you can, and send it to your local board for your file. You should also look at your draft file to see what your local board says about your personal appearance.

The Appeal Process

Once you've submitted your claim to your local board, they will act on it—probably the day or night you appear. If they deny your claim, you should receive a notice of denial, along with a statement of their reason(s). You will have fifteen days from the mailing date of your denial to appeal to the District Appeal Board.

Along with your appeal, if you want it, you should send a request for a personal appearance before the Appeal Board. The postmark on your letter determines whether you have met the necessary deadline.

At the personal appearance before the District Appeal Board, you have some of the same rights as you did when appearing before your local board. You can present evidence to support your claim. And you can have an advisor with you. You have no right to witnesses, however.

Following your appearance before the District Appeal Board, you will again receive a notice of their decision on your claim. If your claim is denied, the Appeal Board must give its reason(s). If the decision of the Appeal Board is unanimous, you have no further appeal.

If one or more members of the Appeal Board disagree with the denial of your claim, you have the right to appeal to "The

President," within fifteen days of the mailing of your notice of denial. Appeals to the President are handled by the National Selective Service Appeal Board. Again, you have the right to request a personal appearance before this board.

When you appear before the National Appeal Board, you again have the right to present evidence to support your claim. And you can have an advisor, just as you did before the local and appeal boards. You again have no right to present witnesses. The National Appeal Board is your final appeal within the Selective Service System.

Induction

If your claim has been denied at all levels, or if you don't request a reclassification, you will be required to report for induction. Your postponement of induction will expire, and you will receive notice of a new reporting date. If you don't report, you will be given another chance to show up, and if you still don't report, you'll be turned over to the Justice Department for possible prosecution.

Induction processing includes a complete Armed Forces mental test, a check of your criminal record (if you have one), and a complete Armed Forces physical examination. If you fail the physical, you will be classified 4-F but you could be re-examined in the future (it's not likely, though). If the military can't determine whether you're qualified for military duty, you could be sent home and called back for re-examination and possible induction in a month or so. If you have a medical condition which should cause you to fail the physical, it's important for you to have proof with you when you go for induction. The military seldom finds conditions if you don't point them out.

If you pass the military examinations, you'll face the choice of accepting or refusing induction. In most cases, you'll have to do one or the other before you can get your case to court. For details, see Chapter 17.

If you've decided to refuse induction, you do so during the induction ceremony. To avoid confusion, it's best to tell the induction center officials in advance that you're going to refuse.

During the induction ceremony, all the draftees being

inducted that day line up and are told to step forward. If you step forward, you become a member of the military. If you don't step forward, you have refused induction. You'll probably be taken aside and given another chance to step forward, warned of the legal consequences of what you're doing, etc. You might be arrested, but this is rare. In most cases, once you've made clear that you aren't going to change your mind, you'll be sent home to wait for prosecution.

If you plan to refuse induction, CCCO recommends that you go to the induction center rather than simply failing to report. It's just possible that you'll fail the physical examination, or that military officials will make an error in your processing that could lead to an acquittal in court. And by going to the induction center, you make sure that you've "exhausted your administrative remedies." The courts require you to do this before they'll hear your case. ("Exhausting your administrative remedies" also includes appealing the denial of your claim.)

If Your Claim Is Accepted

If you make a CO claim and it is accepted, you'll be subject to one of two kinds of duty: noncombatant military duty if you're a l-A-O, or alternative civilian duty if you're 1-0. Noncombatant COs are ordered for induction just like other draftees. To avoid confusion, it's important that you have proof of your noncombatant status when you report for induction. CCCO will issue a detailed update on the status of noncombatants if inductions are reinstated.

Alternative Service

If you're granted 1-0 status, Selective Service will order you to perform two years of civilian work "in lieu of induction" if you would otherwise have been called for induction. Since anyone who applies for reclassification will have been called for induction, and since by this point you'll either have passed an Army physical or waived it, this means in practice that following your successful CO claim you will have to perform two years of civilian work, more commonly known as alternative service. Selective Service will normally expect to place you in an alternative service job within thirty days or less of the time you are finally classified 1-0, so if you want to have a choice of alternative service jobs, you should begin looking as soon as you have filed for CO status, or even before that.

You will be scheduled for an appointment with the Alternative Service Officer (ASO) at a Selective Service Area Office. You will be sent a questionnaire about your education, job skills, and interests. The ASO will then try to match your interests and skills against a computerized job bank.

An alternative service job must be with a government or non-profit agency. It must contribute to the national health, safety, or interest and must employ you at least 35 hours per week. Most COs work in hospitals or other social service agencies, but other options, such as conservation work, may also be available. Jobs with church service organizations will still be among the most attractive, even though they pay poorly, because they will offer better opportunities for meaningful work.

You don't have to take a job from the Selective Service list. You may present your own job on the Selective Service skills form, but you must get your prospective employer's consent, and your prospective employer must agree to Selective Service's terms of employment.

If you can't accept the job to which Selective Service wants to assign you, you have the right to appeal to a Civilian Review Board, whose decisions are officially final. Unofficially, you may find that you can negotiate a better assignment with Selective Service if you are determined and persistent.

Footnotes

Chapter 3

The major cases on conscientious objection are *U.S. v. Seeger,* 380 US 163 (1965); *Welsh v. U.S.,* 398 US 333 (1970); *Sicurella v. U.S.,* 348 US 385 (1955); *Gillette v. U.S.,* 401 US 437 (1971); *In re Nissen,* 146 F.Supp. 361 (1956); *In re Hansen,* 148 F.Supp. 187 (1957); and *Fleming v. U.S.,* 344 F.2d 912 (10th Cir. 1965).

p. 20: *Clay v. U.S.,* 403 US 698 (1971)
p. 20: *U.S. v. Seeger, op.cit.*
p. 21: *Welsh v. U.S., op.cit.*
p. 22: On "religious training," see *Nissen, op.cit.,* and *Hansen, op.cit.*
p. 25: On political beliefs, see *Fleming, op.cit.*

Chapter 4

On selective objection, see *Gillette, op.cit.,* and *Sicurella, op.cit.*
The summary of the Just War theory in this chapter is based on Richard J. Niebanck, *Conscience, War, and the Selective Objector* (Board of Social Ministry, Lutheran Church in America), pp. 39-41.

Chapter 5

A good general summary of the world military situation will be found in Ruth Leger Sivard, *World Military and Social Expenditures.* New York: World Policy Institute, updated annually. (Available from World Policy Institute, 777 United Nations Plaza, New York, NY 10017, for $5.50 postpaid.).

pp. 43-44: For an exhaustive history of NATO and the Cold War, see Richard J. Barnet, *The Alliance: America-Europe-Japan, Makers of the Post-War World* (New York: Simon and Schuster, 1983).

Chapter 6

The chapter represents the author's own conclusions. General sources and ideas for further study are given below.

p. 55: On war and arms races: Laurence Lafore, in *The Long Fuse: An Interpretation of the Origins of the First World War* (Philadelphia and New York: Lippincott, 1965) states flatly that arms races in themselves do not cause wars. A thorough analysis of the pressures and interests which lay behind the Cold War arms races will be found in Alva Myrdal, *The Game of Disarmament* (New York: Pantheon Books, 1976).

p. 56: The discussion of U.S. war plans is based on press reports.

p. 56: There is no standard one-volume history of World War I. A good short history, written from a military commander's point of view, is B. H. Liddell Hart, *The Real War, 1914-1918* (Boston: Little, Brown & Co., 1930). More readable but less complete is Alan Lloyd, *The War in the Trenches* (New York: David McKay, 1976).

p. 56: John Keegan, "Men in Battle," *Human Nature,* Vol. I, No. 6 (June, 1978), p. 36, discussed drilled and "primitive" warfare. A more complete discussion of Keegan's theory will be found in his *A History of Warfare* (New York: Alfred A. Knopf, 1993).

p. 60: On the laws of war see Tom J. Farer, *The Laws of War 25 Years After Nuremberg,* Carnegie Endowment for International Peace pamphlet 583, May, 1971.

p. 61: Military members' right to refuse unlawful orders: Stichman and Rivkin, *The Rights of Military Personnel* (New York: Avon Books, 1977), pp. 103-104.

p. 61: Combat: Books on combat are many, some almost useless. This discussion is based on first-hand accounts in Erich Maria Remarque, *All Quiet on the Western Front,* trans. by A. W. Wheen (Boston: Little, Brown, 1929); Farley Mowat, *And No Birds Sang* (Boston: Atlantic Monthly Press, 1979); and Siegfried Sassoon, *Memoirs of an Infantry Officer* (Riverside, NJ: MacMillan, 1969). A good analysis of combat and human psychology will be found in the works of John Keegan, *op.cit.* Keegan's *The Face of Battle* (New York: Vintage Books, 1977) is also worth reading. The discussion of military training and its effects is based on conversations with many military personnel while counseling them.

p. 64-65: The quote on militarism is from Sidney B. Fay, *The Origins of the World War* (New York: MacMillan, 1928, 1930), p. 39. Definitions not in quotes are from Webster's Unabridged Dictionary.

pp. 65-66: The literature on the causes of war would fill a library of its own. Some suggested readings will be found under "Further Reading" and "A Short Course on War and Peace."

Chapter 7

For a slightly different discussion of modern warfare, see Robert Seeley and Aldoux Huxley, *The Handbook of Non-Violence* (Westport,

CT: Lawrence Hill/Lakeville Press, 1986), pp. 146-153; 162-167; 257-274, among others.

Chapter 8

p. 81: Casualty figures for nearly all wars are estimates only. For the Thirty Years War, see Field Marshall Viscount Montgomery of Alamein, *A History of Warfare* (Cleveland and New York: World Publishing Co., 1968), p. 279. Civil War fitures are official statustics, quoted in Roger Parkinson, *The Encyclopedia of Modern War* (New York: Stein and Day, 1977), p. 7. The ten million figure for World War I is from E. L. Bogars, *Direct and Indirect Costs of the Great War* (1920), quoted in C. R. M. F. Crutwell, *A History of the Great War* (Oxford: The Clarendon Press, 1934), p. 630. World War II figures do not include concentration camp victims. They are taken from Parkinson, p. 149. The Hiroshima figure is from Parkinson, p. 78.

p. 82: Discussion of the size of nuclear bombs is based on The Boston Study Group, *The Price of Defense* (New York: Times Books, 1979), pp. 63-64.

p. 83: The discussion "An H-Bomb in Manhattan," is based on Tom Stonier, "What Would It Really Be Like? An H-Bomb on New York City," in Thomas Merton (ed), *Breakthrough to Peace* (Norfolk, CT: New Directions, 1962), p. 30.

p. 85: LaRocque quote is from Center for Defense Information, *Nuclear War Prevention Kit* (Washington, DC: Center for Defense Information, 1980), p. 3. Quote from Lord Mountbatten is from "On the Brink of the Final Abyss," *Defense Monitor*, Vol. IX, No. 4 (May, 1980), p. 4. All quotes from Mountbatten are from this essay. The definition of "absolute war" is from Parkinson, p. 1.

p. 87: Three essays on nuclear pacifism will be found in National Interreligious Service Board for Conscientious Objectors, *Words of Conscience* (Washington, DC: NISBCO, 1980), pp. 123-124.

Chapter 9

p. 91: Courts on force: *Gillette, op.cit.; U.S. v. Purvis,* 403 F.2d 555 (2d Cir. 1968).

Chapter 8

The major sources for this chapter were: Alan Bullock, *Hitler, A Study in Tyranny* (New York: Harper Colophon Books, 1964); A. J. P. Taylor, *The Origins of the Second World War* (Greenwich, CT: Fawcett, 1961); Peter Calvocoressi and Guy Wint, *Total War: The Story of World War II* (New York: Pantheon Books, 1972); Laurence Lafore, *The End of Glory: An Interpretation of the Origins of World War II* (Philadelphia and

New York: J. B. Lippincott, 1970); Ellen Switzer, *How Democracy Failed* (New York: Atheneum, 1975); John Lukacs, *The Last European War: September 1939/December 1946* (Garden City, NY: Anchor Press/ Doubleday, 1976); and John Keegan, *The Second World War* (New York: Viking, 1989). These are cited below by the author's name.

p. 100: Casualty figures from Roger Parkinson, *The Encyclopedia of Modern War* (New York: Stein and Day, 1977), p. 149.

p. 100: Concentration camp figures are estimates only, from Lucy S. Davidowicz, *The War Against the Jews, 1933-1945* (New York: Holt, Rinehart & Winston, 1975), p. 403, and Calvocoressi and Wint, p. 236.

pp. 101: The leading advocate of the "Hitler's War" theory is Alan Bullock; A. J. P. Taylor took the contrary view.

p. 101-102: On the "German Problem" and the two world wars, see Lafore, p. 11, and Taylor, p. 22, 44.

p. 102: Calvocoressi and Wint, pp. 551-553, give a comparison of World War I and World War II casualty figures.

pp. 102: Taylor, pp. 27-32, outlines the provisions of the Treaty of Versailles. See also D. F. Fleming, *The Origins and Legacy of World War I* (Garden City, NY: Doubleday, 1968), pp. 264-280.

p. 102: On *Freikorps,* see Calvocoressi and Wint, p. 30.

p. 102: Description of the German inflation is quoted from John Kenneth Galbraith, *Money: Whence It Came, Where It Went* (Boston: Houghton, Mifflin, 1975), p. 156.

p. 103: Description of German unemployment is quoted from Switzer, p. 45.

p. 103: Nazi seats in the German parliament: figure quoted from Bullock, p. 169. Hitler's appointment as Chancellor from Bullock, pp. 248-250.

p. 104: Henry Ford's support of Hitler: see Lukacs, p. 252 fn. See also Albert Lee, *Henry Ford and the Jews* (New York: Stein and Day, 1981).

p. 104: Passage from Anne Morrow Lindbergh quoted in Switzer, pp. 153-154.

p. 104: British and French made Munich proposal: Taylor, pp. 146-181.

p. 104: Popularity of "appeasement": Taylor, p. 292.

p. 106: British leaders supporting terms with Hitler: Calvocoressi and Wint, p. 50.

p. 106: Hitler declared war on U.S.: Calvocoressi and Wint, pp. 184-185.

p. 107: Hitler's order to level Germany: Albert Speer, *Inside the Third Reich* (New York: MacMillan, 1970), pp. 561-562.

p. 107: A history of the British part of the "area bombing" campaign will be found in Max Hastings, *Bomber Command* (New York:

Dial Press, 1979).

p. 107: Quote on the effects of area bombing: Calvocoressi and Wint, p. 501.

p. 108: On the willingness of countries to accept emigrant German Jews: Calvocoressi and Wint, p. 238.

p. 109: Establishment of Dachau: Calvocoressi and Wint, p. 228.

p. 109: Quote on American apathy: Arthur D. Morse, *While Six Million Died* (New York: Random House, 1968), p. 383.

p. 110: On the Turkish massacres of Armenians, see Kerop Bedoukian, *Some of Us Survived: The Story of an Armenian Boy* (New York: Farrar, Straus, Giroux, 1978). Figures are quoted from p. 238 of this book.

Chapter 11

p. 117: On Napoleon's invasion of Russia, see R. F. Delderfield, *The Retreat from Moscow* (New York: Atheneum, 1967)

Index

About the Author

Robert A. Seeley is Executive Director of the Philadelphia Office of the Central Committee for Conscientious Objectors. In addition, he is editor of *CCCO News Notes* and supervises CCCO publications.

A native of Philadelphia, he received a B. A. in philosophy from Earlham College in 1965. Following a year with the American Friends Service Committee's National Office, he performed two years' civilian work as a conscientious objector with AFSC in Sumter, S.C.

In September, 1968, he joined the CCCO staff as a draft counselor. In 1973 he was appointed editor of *CCCO News Notes.* From 1974 to 1979, he worked as military counselor and editor of CCCO publications. He was appointed Director of Publications in 1980 and became Executive Director in 1990.

Bob's writing on conscience and war has been published in *The Progressive, Friends Journal, Minerva: A Quarterly Journal on Women and the Military,* among other places. He is author of the *Handbook for Conscientious Objectors* and editor of *Advice for Conscientious Objectors in the Armed Forces,* both published by CCCO, and author of the *Handbook of Non-Violence,* published by Lawrence Hill Books.

About This Book

This book is set in Adobe™ ITC New Baskerville, a digitized version of the traditional text type, Baskerville. Portions were set in Adobe™ Gill Sans. Galleys were prepared on an Apple Macintosh IIsi and Personal LaserWriter NTR, using Aldus™ Pagemaker 4.2, Microsoft Word 5.0, "Index Maker," a custom HyperCard 2.2 application designed by Kalamata Software, and Reports DataPro™ 2.9. Cover prepared using Aldus™ PageMaker 5.0, Aldus™ Freehand 4.0, Aldus™ Super-Paint 3.0, and Broderbund TypeStyler 1.5. Cover graphic by Daniel McClain. Book design by Felicity Productions.